AMERICA:
IDEAL AND REALITY

INTERNATIONAL LIBRARY OF SOCIOLOGY AND SOCIAL RECONSTRUCTION

Editor : Dr. Karl Mannheim

AMERICA:
IDEAL AND REALITY

THE UNITED STATES OF 1776 IN CONTEMPORARY EUROPEAN PHILOSOPHY

by

W. STARK, M.A.,
Dr. rer pol., Dr. jur.

LECTURER IN SOCIAL STUDIES
UNIVERSITY OF EDINBURGH

Les lois sont toujours utiles à ceux qui possèdent et nuisibles à ceux qui n'ont rien : d'où il suit que l'état social n'est avantageux aux hommes qu'autant qu'ils ont tous quelque chose, et qu'aucun d'eux n'a rien de trop.

ROUSSEAU, *Du Contrat Social*, i. 9.

GREENWOOD PRESS, PUBLISHERS
WESTPORT, CONNECTICUT

Library of Congress Cataloging in Publication Data

Stark, Werner, 1909-
  America: ideal and reality.

  Reprint of the 1947 ed. published by K. Paul, Trench, Trubner, London, in series: International library of sociology and social reconstruction.
    1. Social sciences--History. 2. Progress. 3. United States--Civilization--To 1783. I. Title.
H51.S8 1974   309.1'73'03   73-19226
ISBN 0-8371-7313-2

First published in 1947 by Kegan Paul, Trench, Trubner & Co., Ltd.

Reprinted with the permission of Routledge & Keagan Paul Ltd.

Reprinted in 1974 by Greenwood Press,
a division of Williamhouse-Regency Inc.

Library of Congress Catalog Card Number 73-19226

ISBN 0-8371-7313-2

Printed in the United States of America

CONTENTS

CHAP.		PAGE
	Preface	vii
	Introduction: Bourgeois Ideal and Capitalist Reality	1

THE UNITED STATES OF 1776 IN CONTEMPORARY EUROPEAN PHILOSOPHY

I.	The Problem of Europe	14
II.	Raynal the Fatalist	16
III.	Mably the Pessimist	36
IV.	Chastellux the Critic	58
V.	Brissot the Admirer	80
VI.	The Problem of America	101
	Index	111

PREFACE

When I wrote my essay on Saint Simon, since published in the *Journal of Economic History* (New York, May, 1943, and May, 1945), I was struck by an incidental remark of that social philosopher which indicated that he looked upon the early history of the United States as a grand social experiment. The subject at once interested me; I studied it in the early spring of 1941, and the present investigation "The United States of 1776 in Contemporary European Philosophy" was the fruit of my studies. In the following year the Committee of the Marshall Society at Cambridge invited me to read to them a paper on some topic connected with my research, and I chose as my subject a comparison between "Bourgeois Ideal and Capitalist Reality"—the capitalist reality of today which is the natural outcome, and yet the complete perversion, of the bourgeois ideal of the eighteenth century. This lecture, which was delivered in November, 1942, discussed in more general terms the development of which the social history of the United States between 1776 and 1800 furnishes such an impressive illustration; it has therefore been utilized in the present publication as an introduction to the longer investigation together with which it is printed here. The text published below is, incidentally, almost an exact transcription of the lecture. The only difference is that, to illustrate the bourgeois ideal, I had used a number of quotations from Brissot de Warville which are left out here because I wanted to avoid repetitions. The trend of the argument is in no way touched by these omissions.

The subject of these pages has much greater historical and intellectual importance than might appear at first sight. Today left-wing extremists all over the world watch with passionate interest and blind faith the attempt to build a socialist society in the Soviet Union. If their hopes were dashed to the ground, a spiritual crisis would grip thousands and thousands, perhaps millions, and the whole of society would be affected by it. The radicals of 1789 had staked as much on the United States as the communists have on Soviet Russia, and their fond expectations came to nought. In a former book of mine—*The Ideal Foundations of Economic Thought*, also published in Prof. Mannheim's series—I have described the great change of character and outlook which came over political economy when egalitarianism was defeated and class society appeared on the scene. But there was no department of life that was not deeply stirred and decisively transformed. It is a sad story which I have to tell. It confirms the melancholy conviction of Robert Burns that the best-laid schemes of mice and men gang aft agley. An age such as ours, that seems to assume that man is great enough to become master of his fate, may find in it some salutary food for thought.

W. STARK.

EDINBURGH, 1947.

INTRODUCTION: BOURGEOIS IDEAL AND CAPITALIST REALITY

On the 1st of November, 1755, a terrible disaster befell the ancient city of Lisbon. The weather was fine and the sky without a cloud when, shortly before ten o'clock, the whole town began to rock in its foundations. Within fifteen minutes two violent shocks occurred, which reduced many, if not most, of the houses to miserable ruins. At the same time the sea receded so far that the bar of the harbour was laid bare, and then rolled irresistibly back, rising to a height of some 40 feet above its ordinary level. A third great shock completed the destruction of the city.

As it chanced, this earthquake took place on one of the most unpropitious days of the year. For, the 1st of November being the feast of All Saints, there was no church and indeed no house in Lisbon that was not lit up by innumerable candles. As a result fires broke out simultaneously in many parts of the city, and it was not until five or six days had passed that they died down, finding nothing more to devour. And not only the day, but even the hour of the disaster was extremely unfortunate, as it occurred at a time when many people were at their devotions, and all the churches were crowded. This circumstance led to a terrible loss of life, for the heavy stone roofs of the churches and chapels fell in and buried whole congregations before a soul could escape. The number of killed was estimated at about 30,000, but many more were crippled or injured, or fell victims to the flames. When night came the darkness descended on a scene of misery and desolation where only a few hours before there had been a flourishing and contented community.

In our days, when the destruction of cities and the death of thousands is almost an everyday occurrence,[1] such an event as the earthquake of Lisbon is not likely to make a deep and lasting impression. But it was far otherwise in the eighteenth century, when as yet men's minds were not clouded or their hearts turned to stone. The fate of the Portuguese capital, renowned for the

---

[1] This lecture was delivered in the days when the struggle for Stalingrad had reached its climax.

beauty of its situation and the magnificence of its buildings, shocked and distressed all Europe. In fact, the news of the disaster gave rise to an almost universal intellectual crisis, and it was amid this crisis that the fundamental concept of bourgeois society was, perhaps for the first time, clearly conceived and publicly proclaimed.

At the time of which we speak, the whole world of culture was in the midst of a most agreeable dream. The conviction was universal that life was wonderful and its problems anything but serious—passing troubles in a constant system of supreme happiness. Looking back from this, alas ! much more sober century we can well understand the roots from which this optimistic philosophy sprang. In the Thirty Years' War, whose ravages were already forgotten and its wounds long healed, the Middle Ages had died, and men were now witnessing the awakening of a new world. They were living through a period full of promise and anticipation, not unlike those wonderful weeks before spring sets in. For the first time there was real security for all : the towns threw down their walls, the roads were no longer infested by highwaymen, the sea-routes were open to all nations, and such artificial impediments to commerce and industry as rights of staple and guild regulations were visibly, if slowly, passing into oblivion. Religious persecution, too, had been ousted by universal toleration, and there was such a feeling of brotherhood and progress as has never been experienced before or since. The reconstruction of the world according to the principles of enlightened reason and unprejudiced utility seemed at hand.

This sentiment found its classical expression in the philosophical writings of one outstanding genius : Gottfried Wilhelm Leibniz. Although he published only one book in all his lifetime, his ideas spread through all countries with amazing rapidity, and it is not too much to say that, by 1750, his thought dominated educated circles everywhere. In England, not only were Shaftesbury and Bolingbroke his convinced disciples, but, more important still, Dryden and Pope, whose writings are poetic renderings of Leibniz's optimistic deism.

What was the fundamental idea of this great philosopher ? What was the thesis he endeavoured to prove ? His work may, perhaps, safely be described as an attempt to show that there is no real evil in the world. As it has been well put : he sought to justify the ways of God to man. His main treatise, usually quoted as *La Théodicée*, in fact bears the characteristic title : " Essays on the Goodness of God, the Liberty of Man, and the Origin of Evil ".

Clearly, the problem Leibniz set himself is as difficult as the desire to solve it was ambitious. Yet while it is doubtful whether he was able to master it, it is certain that no one could have grappled with it more courageously or more brilliantly. In a materialistic age such as ours his philosophy may sound strange, but there is an inner greatness about it which will always command respect.

The starting-point of Leibniz's thought is the conviction, or rather the assertion, that the whole universe is living throughout ; that there is a soul not only in every man but also in every animal, in every plant, even in every particle of seemingly lifeless matter ; and if the souls of the lower beings are not endowed with consciousness, this does not mean that they are not real, not really existent : they are as real as the human soul when its self-consciousness is set at rest in sleep. These soul-units, these entelechies, Leibniz taught, are not subject to evil of any kind ; they are not exposed to corruption and destruction as are the bodies they animate. All evil has its seat in the body with which the soul is connected, but the soul itself is above and beyond evil. It may of course be asked why the entelechies have been chained by the Creator to parcels of matter, if these are the source of suffering. But, argues Leibniz, it could not be otherwise. We cannot well conceive of a stable order among disembodied, completely free spirits ; their connection with bodies is the guarantee that every soul will occupy, and continue to occupy, that place in the universe for which Providence has seen fit to destine it. Souls, then, are necessarily tied to bodies, and bodies are the carriers of evil of every kind ; but the higher a being's status, the more is it in its power to escape the evil : the more a being can free itself from the physical urges to which it is subject, and follow the command of the moral precepts born of its soul, the more will it rise above suffering and corruption. The highest Being, which is a pure soul unencumbered by any material form, is perfectly happy and perfectly good ; and man can, if he choose, resemble it, at least within certain limits, if only he overcomes his lower nature. This metaphysical doctrine, it is clear, makes evil something unessential and passing, something unnecessary and accidental. And Leibniz taught, indeed, that evil is in its essence purely negative, that it is simply imperfection, the mere absence of good; while the good is eternal, the very essence of things.

But the misery in the world, as Leibniz saw plainly, cannot easily be argued away. From a metaphysical viewpoint it may be described as something negative, but from a physical one, unfortunately, it is experienced as something only too positive. How can we explain pain? How can we justify positive suffering? Why is it necessary, and why has it been included in the plan of creation? Leibniz's answer is this: pain is necessary, positive suffering had to be included in the general plan, because it is the great means for the moral government of the world. It is the punishment which automatically follows the misdeeds of those who rebel against the divine laws. Nature and society are so constituted, or rather have been so contrived by their Maker, that in the ordinary course of things, and without any special interference, good is rewarded by good and evil by evil. Appearances, he admits, are very often at variance with this doctrine: we see bad men prosper and the good sink into misery and despair. But he makes light of this fact. Finite spirits, he says, cannot fathom the order of an infinite universe because their experience is too limited. What we see proves at any rate that the wicked are usually punished and the good usually rewarded according to their merits, and we cannot but conclude that this is the general rule, and indeed the fundamental law of nature. If there are seeming exceptions, they are either such only in appearance, or they are due to some secondary law which we have so far failed to understand.

Thus positive evil is the necessary corollary of human freedom. It is the safeguard which brings back to the royal road to temporal and eternal happiness the man who has strayed from the right path. It may, of course, be asked why God ever endowed his creatures with free will if they constantly abuse their powers and must be constantly coerced into doing what is best for them. But this question leads, according to Leibniz, only to a new and still stronger justification of physical and moral evil. A world of absolutely perfect beings who never err and never sin would be, he contends, the most tedious world imaginable. Sin and suffering have the great function of serving as a contrast to righteousness and felicity: but for them we should not even know what is good. This is a theme of whose variations Leibniz never tires. *La sagesse doit varier*, he says; perfection is not possible without diversity. In one connection he compares the evil in the world to the shadows which every good painter introduces in his pictures because they serve to make the lights more impressive. Elsewhere he likens it to the vinegar which a French cook is wont to use in order to make the food he prepares more palatable : taken alone, vinegar is certainly bad, but if the right dose of it is mixed with the other ingredients, the result is better than if it had been left out. In a third connection he compares it to the beauty-spots which women employ to make their faces more attractive ; they spoil the tiny part they cover, to bring out all the more the beauty of the whole. Thus every evil in the world has a definite mission, and if only we could follow its effects out to the end we should see that it invariably engenders an infinitely greater good. The heinous crime of Sextus Tarquinius was followed by the establishment of the Roman republic, and thus led to the formation of a great polity and the development of all the Roman virtues. Indeed, even sacred history must be viewed in this light. Adam's fault, considered in itself, was a dreadful evil, but it became the occasion of an incomparably greater good, Christ's incarnation ; for who can doubt that the glory of the redemption far outweighs the wretchedness of the fall ?

These considerations lead up to Leibniz's crowning doctrine : that of " the best of all possible worlds ". If it is true that evil was permitted by the Creator only because it helps to enhance the good, it is but logical to take the final step and conclude that things have been so arranged from all eternity as to make the minimum amount of misery subserve the maximum sum-total of happiness. This, indeed, is Leibniz's firm conviction. Before the day of creation, he suggests, God could choose among an infinity of possible worlds. As the perfect being, and therefore of necessity perfectly good, he selected that one which seemed to him to combine evil with good in the most satisfactory way, and brought it into being. The world so created is this world of ours.

Nothing is more characteristic of Leibniz than his attempt to fathom and explain the thought of the Maker before He set to work. " The antecedent and initial will ", he says, " has for its object each good and each evil in itself, detached from all combination, and tends to enhance the good and to check the evil : the intermediate will is directed to combinations, as in the case when one particular good is connected with one particular evil ; and then the will will have some inclination for the combination if the good in it surpasses the evil : but the final and decisive will results from the consideration of all the goods and all the evils which enter into the deliberation, it results from a total combination. . . . Thus the good which God does can only be sufficiently appreciated if its whole extent is considered with regard to the entire universe." Hence, " God has a very . . . strong reason, and a reason very . . . worthy of Him, to tolerate the evils. He not only draws from them greater goods, but he finds them even connected with the greatest good possible : so that it would be a fault not to permit them." Indeed, concludes Leibniz, " to permit the evil [in the world] as God permits it, is the greatest goodness ".

Although this doctrine was in the first place a metaphysical and religious one, it is not difficult to see how it provided the historical background and the intellectual basis for the economic theories of the French physiocrats and the Scottish philosophers. Classical economics has been described, and that rightly, as a proof of the existence of God, and Smith's contention and conviction that the good of all spontaneously results from the selfishness of each is in fact a special application of the general ideas put forward by Leibniz and his followers. But Leibniz himself took an important step forward in the direction of the optimistic social philosophy professed by Quesnay and Turgot, Hutcheson and Smith. He developed the doctrine of the pre-established harmony of which the corresponding teachings of the classical economists down to Carey and Bastiat are only variations. How can it be, Leibniz asked, that the parts composing a whole are truly independent of each other, yet the whole made up of those parts exhibits a perfect order and an unbroken harmony ? How can it be that the men who live together in society are free and selfish, and yet that society constitutes, not a chaos, not a war of all against all, but a cosmos, a picture of peaceful co-operation ? Three answers, Leibniz thought, can in theory be given to these questions. He developed them in an ingenious simile, and we can do no better than follow his example.

Take two clocks, and consider how they can be made to keep time with each other. The first possibility is to connect them by fixing both pendulums to a piece of wood. In this case they cannot but move together step by step. But under such an arrangement their harmony would be secured by the sacrifice of their independence. They would be chained together as men are under a despotic government, where social peace is built on the suppression of individual freedom. The second possibility is the opposite of the first. It supposes that each clock is left to itself. But then small differences will soon appear between the positions of their hands, and it will be necessary to adjust the one to the other at regular intervals. Here the independence of the parts is real, but the harmony of the whole is precarious. This case corresponds to that of a liberal society where the centrifugal forces, let us say the class forces, are stronger than the centripetal, the forces making for social peace. Yet there is still a third possibility, one which realizes at the same time the liberty of the parts and the harmony between them. If the two clocks are absolutely perfect, if their maker has built them so exactly that they are in every respect alike, then they will automatically move with the same speed, and it will not be necessary either to adjust them to each other or to connect them in order to make them keep time. They will do so spontaneously. This, Leibniz taught, is the case of actual society. God has, before all ages, implanted a principle in the human heart which prompts men to live in harmony with each other. Both Smith's *Theory of Moral Sentiments* and his *Wealth of Nations* are attempts to illustrate this thesis and to confirm it.

By the middle of the eighteenth century this thoroughly optimistic philosophy dominated all Europe. In England it had been made popular by Alexander Pope's beautiful *Essay on Man*, whose first epistle admirably sums up the essence of Leibniz's world-view in these words:

> All Nature is but Art, unknown to thee;
> All Chance, Direction which thou canst not see;
> All Discord, Harmony not understood;
> All partial Evil, universal Good:
> And, spite of Pride, in erring Reason's spite,
> One truth is clear: *Whatever is, is right.*

Into this delightful reverie the intelligence of the Portuguese earthquake struck like a thunderbolt out of a clear sky. When the news reached Monsieur de Voltaire, he exclaimed: " Here is a terrible argument against optimism ! " Many must have thought as he, when he asked: " How is this frightful event to be reconciled with the concept of a God whose goodness is unbounded? Could He not have placed us in these dreary climes without lighting volcanoes under our feet? Could the earthquake not have happened in the desert? Or was it meant as a punishment of crimes? What can have been the guilt of the babes in arms who perished at their mothers' breasts? And was Lisbon more wicked than London or Paris? Would it have consoled the victims if philosophers had cry'd out to the wretches who with difficulty escaped from the ruins: 'All this is productive of general good; the heirs of those who have perish'd will increase their fortune; masons will earn money by rebuilding the houses; beasts will feed upon the carcases buried under the ruins, it is the necessary effect of necessary causes'..." Such a reasoning, surely, would have been pure mockery. It was in this vein that Voltaire composed his powerful " Poem upon the Destruction of Lisbon " which he described as " An Inquiry into the Maxim, Whatever is, is right ". The first words characterize the whole; their passionate strength can be felt even in this English translation, poor though it is in comparison with the original:

> Oh wretched man, earth fated to be curst;
> Abyss of plagues, and miseries the worst!
> Horrors on horrors, grief on griefs must shew
> That man's the victim of unceasing woe,
> And lamentations, which inspire my strain,
> Prove that philosophy is false and vain.

It is clear that this attack on optimism, as serious in thought as it was impressive in form, could not long remain unanswered. And, indeed, Voltaire found an opponent who was fully his equal both as philosopher and as artist: Jean Jacques Rousseau. In a " Lettre à Monsieur de Voltaire " of August, 1756, which assumed the dimensions of a little pamphlet, he refuted the arguments against optimism contained in the " Poem upon the Destruction of Lisbon ". It is this letter-pamphlet which, better than anything else, shows how Leibniz's metaphysical philosophy had become the political creed of the rising bourgeois class, and how it was unobtrusively transformed into a practical programme of action. " You would have preferred ", says Rousseau to Voltaire, " that the earthquake should have happened in the desert rather than at Lisbon. Can we doubt that they do happen in deserts? " But there " they do little harm to the animals and primitive men who live widely scattered . . . and have nothing to fear from falling roofs and burning houses ". The existence of positive evil can indeed not be denied, but the question is, what is its cause? Is it the divine order of things? Certainly not. " I see on all sides ", Rousseau writes, " that the evils to which nature subjects us are less cruel than those which we add ourselves." Why blame God and Nature for the misery of Lisbon? " Nature did not collect there 20,000 houses of six or seven storeys, and . . . if the inhabitants of that great town had been dispersed more equally and housed more lightly, the damage would have been much less, and perhaps nil. Everyone would have fled at the first shock. . . . But no ! they must stay, cling to the ruined habitations, expose themselves to new shocks, because what is left behind is worth more than what one may carry away. How many wretches have perished in this disaster because they wanted to take with them their clothes or their papers or their money ? Is it not known that the self of a man has become the least part of him, and that it is [regarded as] hardly worth while saving, if everything else is lost ? "

Rousseau's argument, then, is this : Leibniz's philosophy is not wrong ; on the contrary, it is essentially right. But the whole beneficence of the laws which God has given to His Creation cannot manifest itself today in the social world, because men have developed habits and created institutions which are at variance with those laws and impede their operation. Let men conform to nature, and they will be as happy as Leibniz's philosophy suggests. " You think with Erasmus ", Rousseau says later in his letter, " that few people would like to be born again under the same conditions under which they have lived. . . . Whom have you consulted on this question ? The rich perhaps ; satiated by false enjoyments and ignorant of the true ones [they are] always tired of life and always trembling to lose it. . . . Ask an honest burgher who has passed a humble and quiet life without projects and ambitions ; a good artizan who lives comfortably by his craft ; a peasant . . . in any country . . . where he is free. I dare assert ", Rousseau concludes, " that there is perhaps not a single mountain-crofter in all Haut-Valais who is discontented with his life though it be almost mechanical, and who would not willingly prefer, even to paradise, . . . to be born over and over again " into this world of ours.

These passages from Rousseau's letter to Voltaire show how Leibniz's fantastic metaphysics was transformed into the realistic social doctrine of the third estate. It was transformed by being connected with an essential condition : that society should be organised on a simple, semi-rural basis ; that is should be a community of truly independent members, without rich or poor, masters or slaves ; practically speaking, a commonwealth of peasants and artizans. In such a society the happiness and harmony envisaged by Leibniz would be realized. It would be embedded in the grand scheme of the universe of which order is the keynote, in spite of an incidental seismic disturbance : and—what is most important—the principle of that order would permeate and pacify and perfect all human relationships. Men are equal when they emerge from the hands of nature : in the preservation of their natural equality lies the secret of social felicity. A community where property is evenly distributed—where the social institutions support, and do not disturb, the spontaneous concord of the social forces—a society of equals among equals—would not be visited by clashes and conflicts. No one would be strong enought to suppress his neighbour, and no one so weak as to be forced to submit. The mechanism of an egalitarian community of this kind was classically described by Adam Smith, and it is his work which furnishes the proof that Leibniz's doctrine of a pre-established harmony is true of any society where men are free and not split up into hostile classes.

A commonwealth of peasants and artizans ! A society of equals among equals ! A beautiful dream, but one that could never come true. Two equally inexorable laws forbid its realization : the one technological, the other psychological. The fifty years after Rousseau's death were the fifty years of the industrial revolution : they established the predominance of large-scale industry, and destroyed the foundations of small-scale enterprise on which the social philosophers of the eighteenth century had set their hopes. There is something cogent, something adamant, about the process which led from the bourgeois ideal to capitalist reality. Large-scale industry is technically more efficient than small-scale enterprise : it not only produces more, but it produces more more cheaply. The consequence is an overbearing tendency towards inequality in the sphere of industrial production : the strong have the wind of trade behind them, the weak must make headway against it ; the strong are bound to become stronger, and the weak weaker. Once the slightest difference in riches and ruthlessness makes its appearance (and how could such a difference fail to appear ?) it is sure to go on increasing until society is divided by a rift which can never again be closed. But to the technical weakness of small-scale enterprise is added the psychological weakness of egalitarianism as a principle of social organization. A society could remain egalitarian only if its members preferred equality to inequality, but in fact they never do so. Rousseau and his disciples were convinced that egalitarianism was eminently reasonable and would recommend itself to all men. Even James Mill, certainly no dreamer, suffered under this delusion. As late as 1821 he wrote in his *Elements of Political Economy* : " When a man possesses, what we are now supposing possessed by the great body of the people, food, clothing, lodging, and all other things sufficient not only for comfortable, but pleasurable existence, he possesses the means of all the substantial enjoyments of human life. The rest is in a great measure fancy. The pleasures which can be added to those of which he is thus in possession are comparatively neither numerous nor strong. . . . If the natural laws of distribution were allowed to operate freely, the greater part of the social product would find its way in moderate portions into the hands of a numerous class of persons . . . placed in the most favourable circumstances both for the enjoyment of happiness, and for the highest intellectual and moral attainments. Society would thus be seen in its happiest state." It was a subconscious wish, not rational investigation, which gave birth to this theory and conviction. It is probably true that the accumulation of wealth does not materially increase the enjoyment of life : but the knowledge that one has outdone all others affords a dismal gratification which no human being will easily forego. History, the most convincing arbiter, has decided against Rousseau and Mill : the nineteenth century has seen a triumph of inequality than which none more impressive can be conceived. The bourgeois ideal offered mankind happiness without riches ; mankind has preferred riches without happiness.

It is easy enough now to say that the bourgeois experiment was bound to miscarry. But a sober comparison of mediæval and modern society tends to prove that the latter was, from the outset, foredoomed to failure. In the Middle Ages it was assumed that man is profoundly selfish—which means profoundly bad ; that he will live in peace with his neighbour only if this natural egoism is suppressed ; and that it can be successfully limited only when men are subjected to that great spiritual power which claims to have been instituted by God for the education and salvation of the human race. Modern times think otherwise. Not that the fundamental selfishness of the human beast has ever been seriously denied. But the delusion lies in thinking that it is not dangerous if society is organized along egalitarian lines, for then all men are equally powerful, and it is no longer profitable to hurt a neighbour who can harm me as much as I can harm him. By establishing an equilibrium of forces, the bourgeois philosophers thought they could free the individual from all restraints, and that with impunity. But an equilibrium is, by its very nature, something unstable. Medieval society was like a man whose feet are firmly planted on the soil. Modern society reminds us of a rope-dancer who tries to cross a bottomless abyss on a frail cord, destined sooner or later to lose his always precarious balance. Today we know that it was already upset long ago : we are witnessing the war of the strong for the extermination of the weak, an extermination which is proceeding without mercy and without remorse.

The comparison of bourgeois ideal and capitalist reality, then, reveals one of the greatest tragedies which have ever overtaken the human race—a tragedy so great as to remind us of the one which is said to have fallen on mankind in the beginning of things. Man, placed in the garden of peace and happiness, was allowed to remain there on the sole condition that he kept aloof from the fruit of material gratification, but in that case, as in this, the temptation was too strong for his feeble power of resistance. Too late has he come to realize that his choice was foolish ; thorns and thistles are already growing in his fields. The true social philosopher of our days is not the smiling Leibniz but the gloomy Schopenhauer, the protagonist of pessimism. For Schopenhauer sought to establish, not without success, that our world is the worst of all possible worlds. He did not deny that there are forces in society which make for social harmony, but according to his view they are so weak that they barely suffice to keep men from cutting each other's throats. Yet by preventing the social system from perishing in an atrocious war of all against all, what, he asks, does the good in the world effect save to preserve an order of things which incessantly engenders unlimited misery ? With these convictions, Schopenhauer is the perfect antithesis of the optimist philosopher, and their contrast is characteristic of the contrast between the periods in which they lived. Leibniz taught that there is a minimum of evil in the world which represents a necessary condition of an immeasurable good. Schopenhauer contended that there is a minimum of good which is the basis for the realization of an immeasurable evil.

One more remark and I have done. It seems to me that our own time, which is so eager to advance from capitalism to communism, should learn to look upon the dismal fate of the bourgeois ideal as an earnest memento. For the problem of socialism is essentially the same as that of bourgeois society. It is not allowed us to have at the same time the greatest possible amount of material wealth and the fullest possible realization of social harmony. The maximum of production can be secured only if man's greed and selfishness are given free play; but this must necessarily destroy the ideal of fraternity. The perfection of peaceful co-operation, on the other hand, can only be achieved if the egoistic strain in human nature is successfully curbed, but this again would adversely affect the spring of economic progress. It is a difficult decision with which we are confronted : a question on which science must be silent and the soul must speak. Personally I have no doubt which answer it would be in mankind's interest to give. It was the evil one who offered the Son of Man the treasures of the earth, to turn Him from His sacred mission ; but He was not tempted or troubled, for He knew that there is no salvation for mankind that has not its origin in the human heart.

THE UNITED STATES OF 1776 IN CONTEMPORARY EUROPEAN PHILOSOPHY

CHAPTER I

THE PROBLEM OF EUROPE

When, on the 4th of July, 1776, the representatives of the thirteen insurgent colonies in North America in solemn assembly unanimously declared " that all men are created equal, that they are endowed by their Creator with certain unalienable rights ; that among these are life, liberty, and the pursuit of happiness ", the social order of Europe still rested on the principles of inequality and oppression. In Germany feudalism, with its power of the landlords over the peasants, was still unchallenged as the dominant system of life, and little seemed to suggest that the days of this social constitution were numbered. In England capitalism, democratizing economic and social life, had, by a slow process of development, won the field, but it was left to the next generation consistently to realize the principles of the new epoch. France occupied, historically as well as geographically, an intermediate position. Externally the edifice of the order of the three estates still presented a picture of imposing unity, but internally the forces which were soon to destroy it in a mighty explosion were already at work. Everywhere, however, it was felt that a new period in man's history was about to begin.

To these conditions in the material world those of the world of thought closely corresponded. In Germany Immanuel Kant, in his great system of philosophy, proclaimed liberty and equality the fundamental principles of ethics and politics. In England Jeremy Bentham endeavoured, in a hundred projects of practical reform, to make these same principles the basis of individual and social life. To the French the ideas which were destined to furnish the watchwords of the revolution were neither unattainable ideals nor tried rules of thumb, but guides to a new order of society.

All the enlightened spirits of Europe agreed that the dominion of men over men was evil. But was it possible to replace the old system by a new, the bad system by a good, the system of subordination by a system of co-ordination ? It was not difficult to answer this fateful question affirmatively in theory, but would this faith be able in the future to stand the test of reality?

It was the United States of America which showed hesitating Europe the way from doubt to certainty. Here men were indeed free and equal: the great fact of the feudal order, the monopoly of the soil in the hands of the class of nobles, was unknown. No one was forced perpetually to earn his living as a serf or hireling: whoever felt himself oppressed where he was could go west to begin a life of perfect independence in the almost impenetrable solitudes of a vast continent. However hard the existence of the pioneer might be, it was ideal, for he worked without coercion as equal amongst equals.

No wonder, then, that the social philosophy of Europe was genuinely concerned with the American experiment. Interest in it was alive everywhere, but only in France did it find classical expression. Germany was too far from the New World: works like Cornelius de Pauw's *Recherches philosophiques sur les Américains ou mémoires intéressants pour servir à l'histoire de l'Espèce humaine* (Berlin, 1768–9) regard America almost exclusively from the point of view of the explorer who is out to solve the riddles of an exotic sphere of life. England was too near to the New World: pamphlets like Richard Price's *Observations on the Importance of the American Revolution and the Means of rendering it a Benefit to the World* (London, 1784) approach the problem mainly from the political side, with the intention of showing the colonies' fight for freedom against George III in its right colours. But four great Frenchmen made the new society the object of scientific study and political judgment: Raynal, Mably, Chastellux, and Brissot. In their books the European view of American life is truly reflected.

CHAPTER II

RAYNAL THE FATALIST

Guillaume-Thomas Raynal's *Histoire Philosophique et Politique des Établissements et du Commerce des Européens dans les deux Indes* is not a learned work in the strict sense of the word. Its author, whom enthusiastic contemporaries did not hesitate to rank with Voltaire and Rousseau, and who, according to Edmond Schérer,[1] had greater influence on the approaching revolution than even those most powerful spirits, did not take pains to divide chaff from wheat, error from truth. " The novelist in Raynal is stronger than the historian," says with justice Feugère, his biographer.[2] But what diminishes the value of his work as a piece of historiography increases its value as a document of history. Even though he may have been but the " humble supernumerary of those who were the soul of their time " [3] he nevertheless reflected more strikingly than anyone else the spirit and sentiment of his period. His *Histoire*, which went through twenty legitimate and fifty pirated editions, is for us valuable and interesting precisely because it can be described as the " undigested and incoherent summary of the ideas of Voltaire, Rousseau, and Diderot " [4] and because the " entrepreneur Raynal " employed numerous " commis " such as Pechmeja, Deleyre, Valadier, Thomas, Saint-Lambert, Suard, Guibert, Knyphausen, d'Holbach, Lagrange, Naigeon, La Roque, Martin, Dubreuil, Pestre, and Bonnaterre.

In view of the numerous authors upon whose writings Raynal drew and from whose works he stole for his amazing publication it is not surprising that we find many inconsistencies. Nevertheless, a uniform philosophy of life forms the background of all the discussions. This is apparent from the outset in the investigation of the most important problem of social philosophy which was then the centre of interest and formed as it were the frame within which all special problems of human relations were viewed : the question of the value or vanity of modern civilization.

Raynal, like so many of his contemporaries, undertakes to

---

[1] *Études sur la littérature française au XVIIIe siècle*, 1891, p. 278.
[2] *Un Précurseur de la Révolution : l'abbé Raynal*, 1922, p. 12.
[3] *Ib.*, 85.   [4] *Ib.*, 102.

"examine whether the condition of rude man left to mere animal instinct, who passes every day of his life in hunting, feeding, producing his species, and reposing himself, is better or worse than the condition of that wonderful being, who makes his bed of down, spins and weaves the thread of the silk-worm to clothe himself, hath exchanged the cave, his original abode, for a palace, and hath varied his indulgences and his wants in a thousand different ways ". Raynal seems to answer this question in the vein of Rousseau. " It is in the nature of man that we must look for his means of happiness. What does he want to be as happy as he can be ? Present subsistence ; and, if he should think of futurity, the hopes and certainty of enjoying that blessing. The savage, who has not been driven into and confined within the frigid zones by civilized societies, is not in want of this first of necessaries. If he should lay in no stores, it is because the earth and the sea are reservoirs always open to supply his wants. . . . The savage has no house . . . but his furs answer all the purposes of the roof, the garment, and the stove. He works but for his own benefit, sleeps when he is weary, and is a stranger to watchings and restless nights. . . . He cannot feel the want of what he does not desire, nor can he desire what he is ignorant of. . . . In a word, the savage is subject to none but natural evils. But what greater happiness than this does the civilized man enjoy ? His food is more wholesome and delicate than that of the savage. He has softer clothes, and a habitation better secured against the inclemencies of the weather. But the common people, who are to be the support and basis of civil society, those numbers of men who in all states bear the burden of hard labour, cannot be said to live happy, either in those empires where . . . the imperfection of the police [has] reduced them to a state of slavery, or in those governments where the progress of luxury and police has reduced them to a state of servitude." These last words clearly show how the critique of culture passes into social critique, or rather how the social critique forms the backbone of the critique of culture. However we may draw the comparison between the state of nature and civilization, Raynal holds, there must always " remain a wide difference between the fate of the civilized man and the wild Indian, a difference entirely to the disadvantage of social life. This is the injustice that prevails in the partial distribution of fortunes and stations ; an inequality which is at once the effect and the cause of oppression." There is nothing to counterbalance this evil : " In vain does custom, prejudice, ignorance, and hard labour stupify the lower class of mankind, so as to render them insensible of their degradation ; neither religion nor morality can hinder them from seeing and feeling the injustice of the arrangements of policy in the distribution of good and evil." It is, indeed, in the power of man to change the constitution of state and society. But even a social reform is, in the long run, of no avail : " The mixed governments seem to present some prospects of happiness under the protection of liberty ; but this happiness is purchased by the most sanguinary exertions, which repel tyranny for a time only, that it may fall the heavier upon the devoted nation, sooner or later doomed to oppression."[1]

Hence a comparison between primitive and modern society proves that the development of culture did not increase the happiness of mankind. But, in spite of this statement, Raynal does not arrive at the postulate of Rousseau : *Retournons à la nature !* He is convinced that everything is relative : the state of nature may be proper to natural man, the state of culture is proper to cultural man. " It is to be presumed from what we know of the state of the savages, that the advantage of not being confined by the restraints of our ridiculous cloathing, the unwholesome inclosure of superb edifices, and the complicated tyranny of our customs, laws, and manners, is not a compensation for a precarious life, for contusions received, and perpetual combats engaged for a portion of a forest, for a cavern, a bow, an arrow, a fruit, a fish, a bird, a quadruped, the skin of a beast, or the possession of a woman. Let misanthrophy exaggerate at pleasure the vices of our cities, it will not succeed in disgusting us of those express or tacit conventions, nor of those artificial virtues, which constitute the security and the charm of our societies."[2] This attitude may at first sight appear inconsistent ; it is, however, the expression of a deep and firm conviction, the conviction that any pleasure of the social state is essentially connected with a corresponding pain, any advantage of a certain social order and situation in life necessarily conditioned by an equally great disadvantage. " The more I reflect upon this point," Raynal says in one place,[3] thus exposing to us his considered indifference towards the progress of society, " the more it seems to me, that from the most rude to the most civilized

---

[1] Engl. trans., *A Philosophical and Political History of the Settlements and Trade of the Europeans in the East and West Indies*, London, 1783, VII, 153–8.
[2] VIII, 265 seq.
[3] III, 395.

state of nature, every thing is nearly compensated, virtues and vices, natural good and evil. In the forest, as well as in society, the happiness of one individual may be less or greater than that of another : but I imagine that nature hath set certain bounds to the felicity of every considerable portion of the human species, beyond which we have nearly as much to lose as to gain."

With this indifferent attitude towards the social constitution Raynal connected a fatalistic view of social development. One social order is as good and as bad as any other, and, moreover, the different forms alternate in the course of time, according to unchangeable laws, with brazen necessity : " All civilized people have been savages ; and all savages left to their natural impulse, were destined to become civilized."[1] Thus it was in the past and thus it will be in the future : " In all future ages the savages will advance by slow degrees towards the civilized state ; and civilized nations will return towards their primitive state ; from whence the philosopher will conclude, that there exists in the interval between these two states, a certain medium in which the felicity of the human species is placed. But who is it that can find out this medium ; and even if it were found, what authority would be capable of directing the steps of man to it, and to fix him there ? "[2] It may be possible to conceive an ideal state ; it may even be possible to realize it ; it is impossible to preserve it : " The experience of all nations and of all ages demonstrates, that whatever hath attained to perfection is not long before it degenerates. The revolution is more or less rapid, but always infallible."[3] For " commotions and revolutions are natural to mankind. . . . Ye nations, what are ye in the hands of nature, but the sport of her laws, destined by turns to set dust in motion, and to reduce the work again to dust ! "[4]

Certainly, only when mankind, on its predetermined way, passes into the stage of (political and social) democracy, are men really happy. " It is then, for the first time, that the sacred name of one's country is heard. It is then that man, bent down to earth, raises his head, and appears in his dignity. Then the annals of the nation are filled with heroic deeds. Then there are fathers, mothers, children, friends, fellow-citizens, public and domestic virtues. Then the empire of the laws is established, soars to its extremest height, the sciences arise, and useful labours are no longer degraded." But this realm is founded on sand : " Unfortunately, this state of happiness is only temporary. In

[1] VIII, 18.   [2] IV, 373 seq.   [3] VIII, 317.   [4] VIII, 330 seq.

all parts, revolutions in government succeed each other with a rapidity scarce to be followed. There are few countries who have not experienced them all; and there is not any one which, in process of time, will not fulfil this periodical motion. They will all, more or less frequently, follow a regular circle of misfortunes and prosperities, of liberty and slavery, of morals and corruption, of knowledge and ignorance, of splendour and weakness; they will all go through the several points of this fatal horizon. The law of nature, which requires that all societies should gravitate towards despotism and dissolution, that empires should arise and be annihilated, will not be suspended for any one of them." [1]

The nations with which the annals of mankind are concerned, were generally very famous, but not very happy. "If we read over the history of nations both antient and modern, it will be found, that there is scarce any one of them, the splendour of which hath not been acquired but at the expence of its felicity. People of whom no mention shall have been made in the melancholy annals of the world, must neither have been aggressors nor exposed to attacks; they must not have interrupted the tranquillity of others, nor must theirs have been disturbed by distant or neighbouring enemies.... They must not have been torn to pieces by political factions, nor intoxicated by absurd opinions. The oppression of tyranny must never have drawn tears from their eyes nor excited them to revolt. They must never have delivered themselves from a despot by assassination, nor must they ever have exterminated his satellites, for such are the events which at all times have given a celebrity to nations. On the contrary, in the midst of a long and profound tranquillity, the fields would have been cultivated, some traditional hymns would have been sung in honour of the deity, and the same love songs would have been handed down from one generation to the other. Wherefore must this alluring picture of happiness be chimerical? Because it hath never existed, and if it should exist, it could not possibly be for a long time...." [2]

These words, though they too end in a confession of fatalism, still show that Raynal possessed a certain social ideal, convinced though he was that it would never be more than a beautiful and fugitive dream. He may have found consolation in the reflection that if the absolutely good social order could not be of long duration, neither could the absolutely bad: "No society was

[1] VIII, 19 seq.   [2] VII, 273 seq.

ever founded on injustice. . . . Animated with the spirit of their institution, they would have been eager to raise themselves upon the ruin of each other. No measure would have appeared too odious for this purpose. This would have been realizing the fable of the race engendered from the teeth of the dragon, which Cadmus sowed upon the earth, and which was destroyed as soon as created. How different would be the destiny of an empire founded on virtue ! Agriculture, the arts, the sciences, and commerce, improved under the protection of peace, would have expelled idleness, ignorance, and misery. The chief of the state would have protected the different ranks of men in the state, and would have been adored. He would have understood that not one of the society could suffer, without some injury to the whole body, and therefore he would have attended to the happiness of all. . . . This is what may be called imaginary excellence in politics. These two sorts of government are equally unknown in the annals of the world ; which present us with nothing but imperfect sketches, more or less resembling the atrocious sublimity, or more or less distant from the affecting beauty of one or the other of these great portraits." [1]

Imaginary excellence ! Even if it cannot claim practical importance, it still has theoretical value : as a measure for the judgment of reality, whose changing appearances now resemble more closely the image of good, now that of evil. If we wish to understand the view of the young social and cultural order of the United States held by Raynal as by the *communis eruditorum opinio* of his time, we must discover the ideal which he envisaged for the social life of men. This is no easy task, for—as is obvious from the quotations already made—it is hidden behind a throng of high-sounding declamations. But it is not impossible to grasp its outlines.

A first indication is offered by the chapter in which the Jesuit state of Paraguay is described and extolled : " The people of Paraguay ", we read there,[2] " had no civil laws, because they knew of no property. . . . There was no distinction of stations ; and it is the only society on earth where men enjoyed that equality which is the second of all blessings ; for liberty is undoubtedly the first."

Hence liberty and equality are the basic principles of perfect society. But they prove their strength only if they are united : freedom cannot last without equality : where freedom alone

[1] VII, 277–9. [2] IV, 237 seq.

prevails, the strong soon rise above the weak, the cunning above the simple, the ruthless above the conscientious, and the successful become masters who oppress those to whom success is denied. But even equality is not desirable without liberty : equality kills the will to achievement and makes men passive and indolent. This was evident also in the primeval inhabitants of Paraguay : " The state of equality to which these people were reduced, and from which it was impossible they should raise themselves, expelled every kind of emulation from among them. One Guaranis had no sort of motive to induce him to excel another. . . . It is not enough for the happiness of man, that he should have what is sufficient for him ; he must also have something to bestow." [1]

Ideal, however, as the connection of liberty and equality may appear in theory, it is problematic in practice. For how is it possible to balance the two principles against each other ? As soon as one of them gains the ascendant—and how can that be avoided ?—the evil is there. If equality gets the upper hand of liberty—i.e. if nobody can raise himself above the average— social life stagnates and must rot. This was the case in Paraguay. But if liberty gets the upper hand of equality—i.e. if it is possible for the individual to rise above his fellow-men—the harmony in society becomes untenable and must disappear. This is apparent in the history of civilization. " In the first ages, men were all equals ; but that natural equality did not last long. . . . Before civil societies were formed and polished, all men in general had a common right to every thing upon earth." [2] But " this point of view . . . can only be applied to the primitive state. . . . Is not the nature of property the same every where ; is it not every where founded upon possession acquired by labour, and upon a long and peaceable enjoyment ? " [3] Raynal puts this question only in order to answer it in the affirmative. The ideally best society is obviously impossible ; the problem is to find the best possible society. Is equality to take precedence of liberty or liberty of equality ? Socialism has chosen the first alternative, liberalism the second. Raynal was the mouthpiece of the revolutionary bourgeoisie. There can be no doubt how he cut the Gordian knot. In his eyes the best possible order is the one in which liberty takes precedence of equality : " It hath been said, that we were all born equals ; but that is not true. That we had all the same

[1] IV, 252.   [2] V, 283 ; VI, 54.   [3] *Ib.* 54 seq.

rights. I do not know what rights are, where there is an inequality of talents and of strength, and no guarantee nor sanction. That Nature hath offered to us all the same habitation and the same resources; that is not true. That we were indiscriminately endowed with the same means of defence; that is not true; nor do I know in what sense it can be true that we enjoy the same qualities of body and of mind. There is an original inequality between men which nothing can remedy. It must last for ever; and all that can be obtained from the best legislation will not be to destroy it, but to prevent its abuses. But hath not Nature herself produced the seeds of tyranny, by dealing with her children like a step-mother, and by creating some children weak, and others strong? It is scarce possible to deny this. . . ."[1]

Mankind must submit meekly to this dismal fate. Rebellion against the necessity of nature would call forth the greatest calamities: "The chimerical idea of an equality of stations, is the most dangerous one that can be adopted in a civilized society. To preach this system to the people, is not to put them in mind of their rights; it is leading them on to assassination and plunder. It is letting domestic animals loose, and transforming them into wild beasts. The rulers of the people must be more enlightened, or the laws by which they are governed must be softened; but there is in fact no such thing in nature as a real equality; it exists only in the system of equity. Even the savages themselves are not equal when once they are collected into hords. They are only so while they wander in the woods; and even then the man who suffers the produce of his chace to be taken from him, is not the equal of him who deprives him of it. Such has been the origin of all societies."[2]

If, however, absolute equality is but an unattainable ideal, absolute inequality is a real evil. "The chief basis of a society for cultivation or commerce, is property. It is the seed of good and evil, natural or moral, consequent on the social state. Every nation seems to be divided into two irreconcilable parties. The rich and the poor, the men of property, and the hirelings; that is to say masters and slaves form two classes of citizens, unfortunately, in opposition to one another. In vain have some modern authors wished by sophistry to establish a treaty of peace between these two states. The rich on all occasions are disposed to obtain a great deal from the poor at little expence; and the

[1] VII, 464 seq.   [2] VII, 281 seq.

poor are ever inclined to set too high a value on their labour : while the rich man must always give the law in this too unequal bargain."

Fortunately numerous intermediate forms are possible between the two extremes, perfect equality and irreconcilable class struggle, and the nearer a society which rests on the principle of liberty comes to the principle of equality, the higher must it be valued. It is here that the community has to interfere in order that through its influence inequality may be kept as small as possible. Here lie the possibilities which are open to man in spite of the implacability of the laws of nature : " All legislation, in its nature, should aim at the happiness of society. . . . The wisdom of legislation will chiefly appear in the distribution of property. It is a general rule, which obtains in all countries, that when a colony is founded, an extent of land be given to every person sufficient for the maintenance of a family ; more should be given to those who have abilities to make the necessary advances towards improvement ; and some should be reserved for posterity, or for additional settlers, with which the colony may in time be augmented." [1]

These simple sentences afford us a deep insight into the practical ideal of Raynal and his time. Where the baseness of the old society does not obtain, where the foundations of a new society can be laid, a certain equality is, first of all, to be established by granting every citizen sufficient landed property ; secondly, the postulate of perfect liberty is to be complied with by offering every competent individual the possibility of ascent ; finally, the preservation of this liberty and equality in the future is to be secured by keeping land in reserve to provide for the additional population. It was with these conceptions in mind that Raynal undertook to judge the United States.

If we wished to reduce Raynal's practical ideal of society to a short formula, we might say that he wanted to offer to all the opportunity of beginning the struggle of existence under equal conditions, so that he whose achievement in fact surpasses the average can rise above the average. He did not advocate a social equality which keeps all down to the same level, but " that social equality which does not tend to reduce all conditions and estates to the same degree, but to a more general diffusion of property " [2]—equality in the chances of life, which is easily reconciled with freedom in the pursuits of life.

[1] VII, 428 seq.   [2] VIII, 49.

The proper means for realizing this reconciliation between liberty and equality is obvious : it is the abolition of the right of inheritance. "Can a man who hath ended his career preserve any rights ? Doth he not lose them all when he ceases to breathe ? When the Almighty deprives him of life, doth he not deprive him of every thing that had any relation to it ? Ought his last will to have any influence over the generations which succeed him ? Certainly not. . . . Among the several possible institutions respecting the inheritance of the citizens after their decease, there is one which would perhaps meet with some approbation. This is, that the estates of the deceased should return to the mass of the public funds, to be employed first towards the relief of the indigent, and after that, to restore perpetually a kind of equality between the fortunes of individuals ; when these two important objects had been fulfilled, the rest should be appropriated to the rewarding of virtue and the encouraging of talents."[1]

The state which approached nearest to the realization of these ideas and proved them to be practicable, is China : " In this nation of sages, whatever unites and civilizes mankind is religion : and religion itself is nothing more than the practice of the social virtues. . . . This sublime system of morals, which for so many ages has contributed to the prosperity of the Chinese empire, would, however, probably have experienced an insensible change, if the chimerical distinctions allowed to birth had destroyed that original equality established by nature among mankind, and which ought only to give way to superior abilities and superior merit. In all the states of Europe, there are a set of men who assume from their infancy a pre-eminence independent of their moral character. The attention paid them from the moment of their birth, gives them the idea that they are formed for command. . . . This institution . . . is not established in China, where nobility does not descend by hereditary right. The fame any citizen acquires, begins and ends with himself. . . . In consequence of this perfect equality . . . it is no difficult task to persuade men who are upon an equal footing by birth, that they are all brethren."[2]

In this enthusiasm for the Chinese, Raynal is at one with Quesnay. But in opposition to the physiocrats he does not attribute the welfare of the Chinese people to the predominance of agriculture in the Middle Kingdom. He regarded it as impossible to confine a nation to farming alone : even in this

[1] VII, 81 seq.   [2] I, 156, 164 seq.

respect man must accept the necessary course of development with fatalistic equanimity : " This is the natural and constant proceeding of well-governed states. From agriculture, which is the source of population, they rise to the arts of luxury ; and the arts of luxury nourish commerce, which is the child of industry and parent of wealth." [1]

Even here advantages and disadvantages, good traits and bad, on the whole cancel each other out : "Since manufactures have prevailed in Europe, the human heart, as well as the mind, have changed their bent and disposition. The desire of wealth has arisen in all parts from the love of pleasure. . . . Industry may give birth to vices ; but it banishes, however, those of idleness, which are infinitely more dangerous." [2]

Nevertheless, commerce and industry, if they develop to excess, are not without danger for the happiness of the people. They imply, as experience shows, much greater differences in wealth than agriculture. Therefore they bring forth the tendency to develop greed and covetousness and destroy equality, on which all harmony is founded : " The idea under which we consider property, namely as a source of the increase both of men and subsistence, is an unquestionable truth ; but such is the fate of the best institutions, that our errors will often threaten their destruction. Under the law of property, when it is attended with avarice, ambition, luxury, a multitude of imaginary wants, and various other irregularities arising from the imperfections of our governments, and from the bounds of our possessions, either too confined, or too extended, prevent, at the same time, both the fertility of our lands and the increase of our species." [3]

For this reason it is good to keep trade and industry within certain bounds ; for this reason mankind spontaneously returns to agriculture : " It is a fact somewhat remarkable, though it might naturally be expected, that men should have returned to the exercise of agriculture, the first of the arts, only after they had successively tried the rest. It is the common progression of the human mind, not to regain the right path, till after it hath exhausted itself in pursuing false tracks. It is always advancing ; and as it relinquished agriculture, to pursue commerce and the enjoyments of luxury, it soon traversed over the different arts of life, and returned at last to agriculture, which is the source and foundation of all the rest, and to which it devoted its whole

[1] VII, 404. [2] VIII, 240. [3] IV, 242 seq.

attention, from the same motives of interest that had made it quit it before." [1]

The state must welcome and favour this development, because a *royaume agricole* is socially more uniform and less problematic than a *royaume commerçant* : " The husbandmen deserve to be preferred by government, even to the manufacturers, and the professors of either the mechanical or liberal arts. . . . The government, therefore, should rather be attentive to the support of the country places, than of great cities. . . . In all parts where the people are attached to the country by property, by the security of their funds and revenues, the lands will flourish." [2] It is best, however, if, on a broad agricultural basis, a modest superstructure of manufacture and commerce is created. Then possibilities of rising are given without the menace of too great an inequality between the citizens. " When a people, engaged in agriculture, join industry to property, the culture of their produce to the art of working it up, they have then within themselves every thing necessary for their existence and preservation, every source of greatness and prosperity. . . . The arts multiply the means of acquiring riches, and contribute, by a greater distribution of wealth, to a more equitable repartition of property. Thus is prevented that excessive inequality among men, the unhappy consequence of oppression, tyranny, and lethargic state of a whole people." [3]

The countries of Europe are all far from this ideal. Nearest to it is the small community of Switzerland : " As far as human foresight can penetrate into futurity the state of these people [of the Helvetic body] must be more permanent than that of all other nations. . . . From the top of their barren mountains, they behold, groaning under the oppression of tyranny, whole nations which nature hath placed in more plentiful countries, while they enjoy in peace the fruits of their labour, of their frugality, of their moderation, and of all the virtues that attend upon liberty. . . . Undoubtedly, the love of riches hath somewhat altered that amiable simplicity of manners, in such of the cantons where the arts and commerce have made any considerable progress ; but the features of their primitive character are not entirely effaced, and they still retain a kind of happiness unknown to other men." [4]

Switzerland : Raynal likes this state because it knows no oppression—and no riches. Democracy guarantees the Swiss

[1] VIII, 226 seq.   [2] VIII, 228, 230.   [3] VIII, 236 seq.   [4] VIII, 93.

their liberty, frugality secures them their equality. The life of the Confederates is hard, but happy. Cannot the same be said of the inhabitants of the New World ?

In his discussion of the United States of America Raynal, certainly in full agreement with the revolutionary bourgeoisie surrounding him, implicitly accepted this opinion. In the Confederation of the Thirteen Colonies, precisely as in the Confederation of the Thirteen Cantons, he was convinced, freedom and frugality, that is to say, freedom and equality, prevail. Indeed, equality is even better secured in the New World than in Switzerland, for where there are few men and much land, bondage and inequality cannot easily disturb the social harmony. In contrast to the European without property who is forced to sell his labour-power to an employer and thus gives up all liberty and equality, the American without fortune can move westward to begin in complete independence on new soil a new life founded on property. Therefore, the young communities of the Savannah and Potomac, Rappahannock and Delaware are reminiscent of the golden age which stood at the beginning of the history of mankind : " Societies, in a state of nature, are little numerous ; they subsist of themselves. They separate before a superabundance of population becomes troublesome. Each division removes to convenient distances. Such was the primitive state of the New Countries ; such is that of the New Continent." [1]

But as the development of material riches has begun to disturb the primitive felicity of society in some parts of Switzerland, so has it in some parts of the American Union. This is especially the case in the south. South Carolina " is already the richest of all the provinces . . . Accordingly, the taste for the conveniences of life is generally prevalent, and the expenses are carried as far as luxury. This magnificence was more particularly remarked some time ago in the funerals. As many citizens as it was possible to collect were assembled at them ; expensive dishes were served up, and the most exquisite wines, and the scarcest liquors were lavished. To the plate which the family had, was added that of the relations, the neighbours, and the friends. It was common to see fortunes either much encroached upon, or even deranged by these obsequies." [2]

The consequences of this departure from the old simplicity are most unfortunate. " Men, who prefer the tranquillity of a rural life to the tumultuous abode of cities, ought naturally to

[1] IV, 369.   [2] VII, 356 seq.

be œconomical and laborious ; but this was never the case in Virginia. Its inhabitants were always very expensive in the furniture of their houses ; they were always fond of entertaining their neighbours with ostentation. They always liked to display the greatest luxury before the English navigators, whom business brought to their plantations. They always gave themselves up to that effeminacy, and to that negligence, so common in countries where slavery is established." [1] This last sentence implies the explanation why Carolina and Virginia are farther from Raynal's ideal than Massachusetts and Connecticut : because of the existence of bondage and inequality in the form of slavery. But although this division of the Union was almost as obvious under Washington as under Lincoln, Raynal took little notice of it. Thus it is all the more remarkable that his observations expose the true reasons of the antagonism between North and South which are hidden behind the conflict of abolition.

In the South, as Raynal depicts the conditions, production—and therefore consumption also—are split up : " In Virginia, vessels employed for the exportation of these productions do not find them collected in a small number of staples, as in the other commercial states of the globe. They are obliged to form their cargo by detail from the plantations themselves, which are situated at a greater or less distance from the ocean, upon navigable rivers, of one or two hundred miles in length." The whole territory is entirely rural. " A few small villages only were built. . . . Williamsburg itself hath no more than two thousand inhabitants, though it be the residence of the governor, the place where the national assemblies, and the courts of justice are holden, and where colleges are instituted ; though it be decorated with the finest public edifices on the Northern continent ; and though it be the capital of the colony, since the ruin of James-town." [2]

In the North, on the other hand, production and consumption are concentrated in towns. All New England " except some parts of Connecticut, were originally covered with pine trees ; and, consequently, are either entirely barren, or not very fertile. . . . Their produce hath never been sufficient for the nourishment of its inhabitants. . . . Accordingly . . . the country places are not the most interesting part of those regions. It is upon coasts surrounded with rocks, but which are favourable to fishing, that the population hath augmented, activity hath increased, and easy circumstances are become general. This

---

[1] VII, 339. [2] VII, 338 seq.

insufficiency of the harvest ought to have excited industry in New England sooner, and more particularly, than in the rest of the continent. . . ." Shipbuilding, hat manufacture, the production of cloth from flax, hemp, and wool, the distilling of molasses here reached a flourishing state. "The greatest resource of those provinces, however, always was the fishery, which was very considerable." [1] In accordance with this economic character of the four colonies, their capital, Boston, is of a strictly industrial stamp. "The houses, furniture, dress, food, conversation, customs and manners, were so exactly similar to the mode of living in London that it was scarce possible to find any other difference, but that which arises from the greater numbers of people there are in large capitals." [2]

If we compare these two descriptions we recognize not only that the North was much more industrialized than the South, but also that even the agriculture of the South was essentially different from that of the North. The agriculture of the South produced for export, that of the North for the home market. The latter sold its produce in a near, the former in a distant market. Or, to employ Thuenen's language and to describe the facts more exactly, the agriculture of the South belonged to one of the outer, the agriculture of the North to one of the inner circles of Thuenen's scheme. Consequently intensive cultivation, small-scale production worked by the peasant family, was proper to the North, and extensive, that is to say large-scale production with cheap labour, to the South. In the plain words of the slave-owner quoted by Montesquieu : " Sugar would be too dear if the plants which produce it were cultivated by any other than slaves " [3] lies the whole explanation of the development which found its dramatic solution in the years 1861–5 and completely dominated the early history of the United States.[4]

[1] VII, 249 seq.   [2] VII, 256.
[3] *The Spirit of Laws*, ed. Prichard, 1878, I, 257.
[4] To develop and prove this thesis fully, an independent investigation would obviously be necessary. Here I cannot do more than put the problem and hint at its solution. In the meantime I refer to my publications : " Ursprung und Aufstieg des Landwirtschaftlichen Grossbetriebs in den Böhmischen Ländern " (*Veröffentlichungen der Prager Universität*, Heft 7, 1934) ; "Niedergang und Ende des Landwirtschaftlichen Grossbetriebs in den Böhmischen Ländern " (*Jahrbücher für Nationalökonomie*, 1937). What, it will be asked, have the Bohemian countries in common with the United States ? Very much indeed. Both were at that time in the same position with regard to agriculture. Virginia and Carolina produced for the centre of consumption in Western Europe (London, Amsterdam) in the same way as did Bohemia and Moravia, and although the latter's geographical distance from the Channel is less than that of the former, their economic distance was then practically equal, for it was more expensive to transport the produce of Bohemia than that of America.

The essential difference between the Northern and the Southern states which Raynal had so well grasped, shows that it was impossible to speak of a perfect uniformity in American society. This appears also in his social analysis of the American population : " While tyranny and persecution were destroying and exhausting population in Europe, English America was beginning to be filled with *three sorts of inhabitants* " we read. " The *first class*, which is the most numerous, consists of freemen. . . . The *second class* of colonists was formerly composed of malefactors which the mother-country transported, after condemnation, to America, and who were bound to a servitude of seven or fourteen years to the planters who had purchased them from the courts of justice. These corrupt men . . . have been replaced by indigent persons, whom the impossibility of subsisting in Europe has driven into the New World. . . . Having embarked without being able to pay for their passage, these wretched men are at the disposal of their captain, who sells them to whom he chuses. This sort of slavery is for a longer or shorter time ; but it can never exceed eight years. . . . At the end of his servitude, the contracted person enjoys all the rights of a free citizen. . . ." The *third class* are of course the slaves : " Yes, by an antiquity, the more shocking as it is apparently the less necessary ; the . . . provinces have had recourse to the traffic and slavery of the Negroes. It will not be disowned, that they may be better fed, better clothed, less ill-treated, and less overburthened with toil, than in the islands. The laws protect them more effectually, and they seldom become the victims of the barbarity or caprice of an odious tyrant. But still, what must be the burthen of a man's life who is condemned to languish in eternal slavery ? " [1]

This recognition of three social strata seems at first to put Raynal in opposition to the dominant opinion of his time, which held that America knew no class contrasts. But he was not far from this view. The temporary slave, who must pay his passage by bond work, by lapse of time automatically becomes free, and then has the same possibilities of independence and becoming rich as anyone else. The black man is indeed worse off. But even he can, and one day will, be helped.

The solution of the problem of slavery, Raynal thought, would be brought about in two ways : by the removal first of the economic, and then of the racial disadvantages. Both,

[1] VII, 406, 408 seq., 414 seq.

however, demand time. " The great benefit of liberty must be preserved for their posterity. . . . These children, till they attain their twentieth year, should belong to the masters of the manufacture or plantation where they were born, in order that he may be reimboursed the expences which he will have been obliged to incur for bringing them up. The five following years they should still be obliged to serve him, but for a stipulated salary settled by the law. After this time they should be independent. . . . A hut should be given to the new citizens, with ground sufficient to make a small garden, and the treasury should be at the expence of this establishment. No regulation should deprive these men, become free, of the power of extending the property which shall have been gratuitously bestowed upon them." [1]

If this were done the inequality in property would be removed. But even the inequality in colour should and could be removed also. " How greatly might the improvements of the . . . provinces be accelerated, if the new sovereigns of North America would depart from the maxims they have uniformly pursued, and would condescend to intermarriages with Indian families! And for what reason should this method of civilizing the savage tribes, which has been so successfully employed by the most enlightened politicians, be rejected by a free people, who, from their principles, must admit a greater equality than other nations ? " [2]

In spite of temporary and even hereditary slavery, the United States of America is therefore a home not only of liberty, but also of equality. Indeed, if only the free settlers are taken into account, who, after all, constitute the overwhelming majority of all inhabitants, the new communities can be regarded as a real approximation to the ideal.

In America liberty and equality are facts, not words : " Dispersed over an immense continent, free as nature, which surrounds them, amidst the rocks, the mountains, the vast plains of their deserts, and on the skirts of those forests, where every thing is still wild, and where nothing calls to mind neither the servitude nor the tyranny of man, they seem to receive from natural objects lessons of liberty and independence. Besides, these people, who are almost all of them devoted to agriculture, to commerce and to useful labours, which elevate and strengthen the mind by giving simplicity to the manners, who have been hitherto as far

[1] V, 305 seq.   [2] VII, 382.

removed from riches as from poverty, cannot yet be corrupted either by an excess of luxury or by a multiplicity of wants." [1]

This state is, as we have seen, in Raynal's eyes the happiest through which mankind can ever pass. And even the legislation of the States is, on the whole, as good as is possible in view of the imperfection of all things human. Pennsylvania may serve as a model : " Penn's humanity . . . extended itself to all those who were desirous of living under his laws. Sensible that the happiness of the people depended upon the nature of the legislation, he founded his upon those two first principles of public splendour and private felicity, liberty and property. If it were allowed to borrow the language of fable, with respect to an account that seems to be fabulous, we should say, that Astraea, who had been gone up into heaven for so long a time, was now come down upon earth again, and that the reign of innocence and concord was going to be revived among mankind." [2] In spite of the predominance of the principle of liberty, provision is made that the principle of equality is not totally lost. " Virtue had never perhaps inspired a legislation better calculated to promote the felicity of mankind. . . . All the laws, that they might have no vices to punish, were calculated to put a stop to them even in their very sources, poverty and idleness. It was enacted that every child above twelve years old, should be obliged to learn a profession, let his condition be what it would. This regulation, at the same time that it secured the poor man a subsistence, furnished the rich man with a resource against every reverse of fortune, preserved the natural equality of mankind, by recalling to every man's remembrance his original destination, which is that of labour, either of the mind or of the body." [3] In Pennsylvania you do not find, as in Europe, immense riches and unspeakable poverty side by side : " There is a constant plenty, and an universal appearance of easy circumstances. . . . The pleasing view of this abundance is never disturbed by the melancholy appearance of poverty. There are no poor in all Pennsylvania. All those whose birth or fortune have left them without resources, are suitably provided for." [4]

Can there ever be a greater felicity than that prevailing in the United States ? " It is in the colonies that men lead such a rural life as was the original destination of mankind, best suited to the health and increase of the species : probably they enjoy all the happiness consistent with the frailty of human nature.

[1] VII, 449. [2] VII, 289. [3] 291 seq. [4] 298 seq.

We do not, indeed, find there those graces, those talents, those refined enjoyments, the means and expence of which wear out and fatigue the springs of the soul, and bring on the vapours of melancholy which so naturally follow the disgust arising from sensual enjoyment ; but there are the pleasures of domestic life, the mutual attachments of parents and children, and conjugal love. . . . This is the enchanting prospect exhibited throughout North America. . . . The female sex are still what they should be, gentle, modest, compassionate, and useful ; they are in possession of those virtues which perpetuate the empire of their charms. The men are engaged in their first occupations, the care and improvement of their plantations, which will be the support of their posterity. One general sentiment of benevolence unites every family. Nothing contributes to this union so much as a certain *equality of station*, a security that arises from property, hope, and a general facility of increasing it ; in a word, nothing contributes to it so much as the *reciprocal independence* in which all men live, with respect to their wants, joined to the necessity of social connections for the purposes of their pleasures. Instead of luxury, which brings misery in its train, instead of this afflicting and shocking contrast, an universal ease, wisely dealt out in the original distribution of the lands, has by the influence of industry given rise in every breast to the mutual desire of pleasing ; a desire, without doubt, more satisfactory than the secret disposition to injure our brethren, which is inseparable from an extreme inequality of fortune and condition." [1]

This social peace is fit to become the fostering soil of a great cultural bloom : " Why should not Athens and Lacedæmon be one day revived in North America ? Why should not the city of Turnbull [in Florida] become in a few centuries the residence of politeness, of the fine arts, and of eloquence ? The new colony is less distant from this flourishing state than were the barbarous Pelasgians from the fellow citizens of Pericles." [2]

Thus even Raynal, convinced as he was that everything perfect is destined soon to perish, cast a favourable horoscope for the United States. But in the admonition directed to the citizens of the new commonwealth there is yet a serious undertone which makes it obvious how accurate was his foreboding of the problems of the future : " People of North America, let the example of all the nations which have preceded you, and especially that of the mother-country, serve as a lesson to you.

[1] VII, 421 seq.   [2] VII, 380.

Dread the influence of gold, which, with luxury, introduces corruption of manners and contempt of the laws. Dread too unequal a repartition of riches, which indicates a small number of wealthy citizens, and a multitude of citizens plunged in misery; from whence arises the insolence of the former and the degradation of the latter. . . . Let liberty have a firm and unalterable basis in the wisdom of your constitutions, and let it be the everlasting cement which connects your provinces together. . . . And may your duration, if possible, be long as that of the world!" [1]

[1] VII, 563 seq.

CHAPTER III

MABLY THE PESSIMIST

Gabriel Bonnot de Mably belonged to the same intellectual circle as Guillaume-Thomas Raynal. He too endeavoured to fathom the secret of social felicity, and he too was convinced that he had found it in the formula of the free play of equal forces. But—contrary to Raynal, as to the prevailing opinion of his time—his solution of the conflict between the ideals of liberty and equality declared equality to be the first of values and assigned to liberty only the second place. " Independence and equality, both, it is true, are gifts of nature, but they are different, and they were given to us for different ends ; we were not created as equals because it was essential that we should remain independent ; but we were born independent because it was essential for us to be born equals and to remain in our equality." [1] This attitude is fundamental to all Mably's work : " The whole burden of Mably's thinking ", Laski rightly says, " is the insistence that, since men think differently who live differently, a state built upon serious inequality can never have that unity of interest upon which a well-ordered commonwealth depends." [2]

Natural law and natural order are for Mably the law and order of equality : " Equality is necessary to men. Nature made it a law for our earliest ancestors and declared her intentions so clearly that it was impossible to ignore them. In fact, who could deny that, emerging from her hands, we found ourselves in the most perfect equality ? Did she not give to all men the same organs, the same wants, the same reason ? Did not the goods she spread over the earth belong to them in common ? Where can you find a principle of inequality ? Did she grant to every one a fortune of his own ? Did she place boundary stones in the fields ? She did not then create rich and poor." [3]

However far mankind may have moved from the original equality in the course of history, it is today still apparent that it represents the first commandment of nature : it is apparent

---

[1] *Œuvres complètes de l'abbé de Mably*, 1793, XII, 59.
[2] Introduction to Whitfield's *Gabriel Bonnot de Mably*, 1930, xi seq.
[3] XII, 49 seq.

in each human being that enters upon this world : " I am strongly inclined to believe that, at their birth, all children are alike. Having as yet no idea (for nobody now believes in the innate ideas of Descartes and Malebranche), and being restricted to trying their soft, delicate, and hardly formed senses, they do not yet feel in themselves the germ of any of those passions by which they will soon be agitated."[1]

But not only with regard to their emotions, even with regard to their intellect all men are equal at birth : " The needs of our first forefathers were too simple for their inclinations to be . . . varied. . . . I say the same for the talents ; nature does not deal them out with so much inequality that they might establish a great difference in the condition of men. It is our education, so capable of stupefying some, and developing in the others the faculties of their mind, which persuades us that providence has made different classes of men."[2]

This education to inequality is in opposition to nature ; so is the whole fact of inequality. Modern society is therefore unnatural, and that means—Mably here proves himself a genuine child of the age of Rousseau—evil : " The more I reflect upon it ", he says, " the more am I convinced that the inequality of fortunes and conditions decomposes man, so to speak, and corrupts the natural sentiments of his heart. . . . I believe that equality, upholding the modesty of our demands, preserves in our soul the peace which withstands the birth and progress of passions. . . . Equality must produce all good because it unites men, elevates their souls, and prepares them for mutual sentiments of benevolence and friendship ; hence I conclude that inequality produces all evil because it degrades and humiliates them and sows among them discord and hatred."[3]

But is it not unjust to accuse inequality ? Is it not the source of many blessings, even though it is the source of many evils as well ? Has it not its just origin in the fact that the competent— he who fosters the material well-being of mankind—receives higher wages for his labours—for his achievements—than the incompetent ? Mably is well aware of this truth. But he is of the opinion that the material advantages of the system of liberty do not counterbalance its ideal and moral disadvantages. " Even if private property in land were much more favourable to the reproduction of riches than it really is, it would still be better to prefer community of goods. Of what avail is that greater

[1] XV, 140.   [2] XII, 55 seq.   [3] XII, 43 seq.

abundance, if it induces men to be unjust and to arm themselves with force or fraud in order to enrich themselves? Can we seriously doubt that in a society where avarice, vanity, and ambition were unknown, the last citizens would be happier than our richest landlords are today?"[1]

In opposition to the socialists of later times who believed, and refuse to give up the belief, that it is possible to combine the productivity of capitalism with the justice of communism, Mably openly faced the irreconcilable contrast between liberty and equality. He was well aware that the realization of the ideal of equality and justice demanded the partial abandonment of the ideal of liberty and productivity. But he did not hesitate in making his choice. For is material well-being the highest of all values? " Riches . . . can at best procure a passing pleasure such as is given by the deceitful caresses of a courtesan, and passing pleasures are not happiness. . . . Happiness in any individual is the peace of the soul."[2] It is his deepest conviction as a philosopher which is expressed in these words : " Happiness is in us and not in the objects that surround us."[3]

In order to enjoy the higher benefit of inward happiness, it is necessary to forsake the lower benefit of external welfare. Mably is—if we may so put it—an ascetic utilitarian. An harmonious social life for men is possible only if they submit to certain postulates of practical philosophy, and " the first of these virtues is temperance . . . Great riches are so useful to so many different passions and so useless for the realization of virtue and happiness that, if they are not a great evil in themselves, I cannot help regarding them as the source of a great evil ; for they incite, arouse, enflame all the passions, and it is impossible always to fight and never to be conquered."[4]

This truth must also serve to guide the politician : " What then is the happiness which politics should propose as its aim? Monseigneur, it is [material] mediocrity. . . . The majority of men are miserable only because they stupidly despise the felicity which nature has laid in their hands in order to run after chimeras which their passions present to them. They search with pain and far from themselves what they would surely find in themselves, if they would only know the value of mediocrity. Could Nature, who wishes to unite men and whose object it certainly is to make them happy through one another, attach happiness to any other condition than mediocrity, the proper

[1] XVI, 16. [2] XIV, 90. [3] XV, 65. [4] XV, 99.

virtue of which it is to moderate and . . . to satisfy our needs at little cost ? " [1]

To secure these social morals, the social morals of the renunciation of riches, must therefore be the kernel of all the endeavours of the legislator. " It would be strange politics if a legislator was persuaded that it is sufficient to make laws in order to secure their being obeyed. He has done nothing if he has only circumscribed the rights of citizens and set fixed limits to justice. If you allow our passions to work they will soon have burst these bounds. . . . Virtue ties men together by inspiring them with mutual confidence." [2]

Virtue—manners : it is always the renunciation of riches which Mably regards as the basic condition of a harmonious society—the renunciation of riches which is to secure the benefit of equality. Mably goes so far as to believe that a poor nation is more likely to be happy than a rich one. " Men ", he says, " are more fitted to resist misfortune than prosperity." As Diogenes was happier than Alexander because he possessed the peace of equanimity, the peace of soul, which the latter lacked, so a people living in frugality is happier than a people who indulge in luxury, because they call social peace, the peace of equality, their own.

Thus Mably not only makes the sacrifice of productivity on the altar of equality, he even, quite logically, makes the restriction of riches his programme. The state which, in his view, came nearest to social equality, because it united equality and frugality, was Sparta. It is Sparta which he presented as the model to his time.

" In order to make the citizens worthy of being truly free, Lycurgus established perfect equality in their fortunes ; but he did not restrict himself to making a new partition of the soil. Since nature had obviously not given to all Lacedæmonians the same passion, nor the same skill in making the best of their heritages, he feared lest avarice should soon accumulate possessions ; and so that Sparta should not enjoy a merely passing reform he descended, so to speak, into the very depth of the hearts of the citizens and there stifled the germ of the love of riches." This wisest of all legislators well knew that in the love of riches he would strike at the propensity to evil.

" Lycurgus proscribed the use of gold and silver and introduced iron money as a medium of circulation. He established

[1] XVIII, 76, 81. [2] XIV, 106 seq.

public meals where every citizen was forced to give a continuous example of temperance and austerity. He wished that the furniture of the Spartans should be manufactured with hatchet and saw ; in a word, he restricted all their wants to those which nature indispensably demands. From that time the arts which serve luxury abandoned Laconia : riches, having become useless, appeared contemptible, and Sparta became a fortress inaccessible to corruption."

Hence equality cannot persist without the renunciation of riches ; but renunciation of riches, on the other hand, is without value if it is not supported by equality. This was proved by the history of the Republic of Geneva. "Calvin did not fail to make sumptuary laws ; but . . . he did not sufficiently know the human heart and the trend of the passions. . . . After the political equality of the citizens had been shaken by the inequality which had become established in their fortunes, nothing did more honour to the wisdom of the Genevese than the tranquillity which they continued to enjoy ; and undoubtedly it must be attributed to the sumptuary laws. . . . Riches, however, had not entered Geneva with impunity, and that leaven of discord and dissension was bound to ferment. . . . In the end quarrels broke out. . . ."[1]

Equality and renunciation of riches are therefore the true foundations of public welfare, and they mutually condition each other : "If I establish equal citizens who consider in men only virtues and talents, emulation will be confined to the right limits. Destroy that equality, and instantly emulation will turn into envy and jealousy, because it will no longer set itself an honest aim."[2]

Hence in the end, as is obvious from these words, Mably, like Raynal, conceived the problem of public welfare as a problem of equilibrium. Raynal had taught that the principle of liberty must be completed and balanced by the principle of equality, if it is not to change from a blessing into a curse for humanity. Mably teaches that the principle of equality must be completed and secured by the principle of renunciation of riches, if it is to endure and to unfold its beneficial effects. But was an equilibrium of this sort possible ? And, if so, was it (at least as things were) possible for any length of time ? Mably answered these questions differently : the first in the affirmative, the second in the negative. In the beginning of human history, in the childhood of the human race, it was realized ; but it was not long before it was lost.

[1] XII, 142-4.   [2] XII, 44.

It was the introduction of private property which led to the fall of ideal society.

"Nothing appears to me to have been easier than to keep men within their duty before property had been established; for nothing was easier than to provide for their needs, and to satisfy them.... I see everywhere public stores where the riches of the republic are contained; and the public functionaries, true fathers of the country, have hardly any other task than to uphold manners and to distribute to each family the things which they need."[1] Then liberty showed its beneficial side: social harmony. But its great disadvantage became equally obvious: the lack of emulation led to economic stagnation.

"It is apparently laziness which troubles the happiness of this golden age. Perhaps some people more indolent and less active than the others who expected their subsistence from the common work of society served [the common cause] with less assiduity and zeal." It was evidently necessary to introduce a stimulus. It was necessary to combine the principle of equality of wealth with the principle of liberty of ascent in order to awaken and keep alive the will to work in all citizens. But could not this be done in a way which achieved its aim without sacrificing equality to liberty?

"A thousand means, each simpler than the other, presented themselves to . . . our fathers, all equally fit to maintain order. . . . To banish laziness it was necessary only to encourage industry by making laws that would awake in the citizens the natural instinct which induces us to seek the esteem of our neighbours and to fear their contempt. To stop the complaints of the hard-working men who found it bad to work for citizens useless to society, it would have sufficed to grant them rewards and distinctions by which they would have been regarded as the benefactors and fathers of the fatherland." Unfortunately, this way was not chosen: instead of starting from the social desire to be esteemed by one's fellow-men on the basis of higher achievements, the a-social tendency was unchained to distinguish oneself from one's fellow-men by greater riches.

"Since we no longer live from the spontaneous produce of the earth, the most industrious citizens argued, and since the work of our hands is necessary to society, it is just that each citizen should contribute in an equal degree. There is only one means of banishing laziness and punishing the lazy; in future

[1] XII, 71 seq.

let the produce of the earth belong only to those who have cultivated it. . . . Let us make an equal division of our lands; then necessity, the most powerful of laws, will banish laziness; want will impart force, activity and industry. . . . They did not discover the abyss which they dug under their feet, and they resolved upon the dismal law which ordained the partition of the soil." [1] This act was the turning-point from good to evil: the fall from the happiness of paradise into the misery of the present. As soon as private property—which means the principle of inequality—was in the world, society rapidly began to split into two hostile camps:

"Inequality in wealth cannot exist without there being rich people, and consequently poor. Will not these sell their services to the others, and will not their souls be humiliated? Let us not judge these beginnings of corruption by the minor abuses which it produces at first, but by the unfortunate future which it heralds. The wish to set limits to what is bad, said one of the greatest men of Antiquity, is like the pretension of a fool who jumps from the rock of Leucate that he will be free, if he so wishes, to maintain himself in the middle of his fall. However little one may deviate from reason, the passions push on and advance extremely quickly. Once we begin to obey them, we delight in no longer resisting them: Cicero is right, and our evils are without remedy." [2]

Our evils are without remedy: in these words lies the key to Mably's whole social philosophy. He proclaimed a loftier ideal than his contemporaries, but he contented himself with a more wretched reality. He thought out a society of highest felicity, but regarded as possible only a society of mitigated evil. The introduction of private property occupies the same place in his social thought as does the fall of man in Christian theology. But he did not believe in redemption: once the right way is left, he was convinced, the high aim can no longer be attained. Once humanity has given up the principle of fraternity, it is for ever a prey to the curse of hate. This terrible fact cannot be changed:

"When equality no longer exists, when the citizens have divided out the lands, when the community of goods can no longer be re-established, what then, you will ask me, is the task of a legislator? He should imitate a pilot whom contrary winds imperiously turn away from his course. He does not submit to

[1] XII, 74. [2] XII, 45 seq.

their fury, he tacks, he sets his sails in such a way that he keeps as near to it as possible. The passions to which property has given rise are in states what the winds are on the sea ; do not set yourself against them, they will carry you away, you will be submerged." [1] The conquest of the evil is not possible ; one must submit to it. In this way the theoretical communist turns into a practical capitalist :

" It seems to me that the first passion which property has given to us, is avarice ; it is this, unless I am mistaken, from which flow all our vices and all our misfortunes ; hence it must be attacked. But this furious passion acquires new forces in the struggle ; the more it has to fear, the more audacious it becomes, and in the end it always gains the victory. . . . The first consequence which I draw . . . is that in all states where property is once established, it must be regarded as the foundation of order, of peace and of public security." [2]

The golden age of earthly happiness is gone for ever, definitely and irrevocably : " Once this folly of the partition of goods has been committed, men are unfortunately condemned to be eternally its victims. . . . No human force could try today to re-establish equality without causing disorders much greater than those which one wishes to avoid." [3]

With this profound scepticism, and indeed pessimism, with regard to social development in the present and the future, Mably combined a profound scepticism and pessimism with regard to the individual man of today and tomorrow. He was, in fact, as Whitfield rightly says,[4] " a misanthropical philanthropist ". The man of his environment seemed to him so corrupted by experience and education of class society, that he was not even capable of grasping his true interests : " If one presented to men the true order of nature, which, according to my view, consists in the community of goods, and the equality of stations, I admit quite frankly that it would not make any impression on their minds ; insurmountable barriers separate us for ever from that happiness." [5] But even if one could today give men the ideal society, even if one were capable of realizing the social order which contains the greatest possibilities of felicity, nothing would be achieved :

" If by dint of eloquence and demonstration, granting this ridiculous supposition, one could work the miracle of reducing

---

[1] XII, 102 seq.   [2] XII, 103 seq.   [3] XVI, 15.
[4] *Op. cit.*, 25.   [5] XVI, 47.

the great and rich to contenting themselves with an entire equality with the people whom they despise, I do not know whether the petty and poor would consent, or, at least, whether they could assume sentiments conforming to their new situation. . . . In almost all Europe things have come to such a degree of meanness and misery that they would show a sort of reluctance and feeling of shame in equalling the others and would find themselves embarrassed on their side." [1]

From all this it follows that to attempt to foster the happiness of society by positive means would be senseless. It can be increased only in a negative way : by restraining the inexterminable evil as far as possible. "We should like the good without mixture, and still it is a great folly to hope for it, since society is only composed of men, that is to say, of very imperfect material. Let us content ourselves with that sort of perfection which nature has permitted us to attain, and with the means she has given us to reach it : the smallest evil—that is our greatest good." [2]

Hence, even if we cannot secure the good of equality, we can at least fight the evil of inequality. "If we cannot aspire today to the equality of Sparta, if we cannot assign an equal patrimony to each citizen, it is at least easy to banish mendicancy and excessive opulence from a state. It is easy to establish an order of things such that labour would furnish every man with an honest subsistence, and that there should be no circumstances in which an industrious father with his family should be condemned to die of hunger." [3]

In order to reach this economically and socially very modest aim, it is necessary to bring about first of all the equalization of all citizens before public law and in public esteem : "The equality to which men are still permitted to aspire and which must necessarily be established is in essence that in society no man should be freed by birth, title or privilege from the duties of citizenship, and that the quality of citizenship should be invariably respected [even] in the least man in the state. Since we do not know how to be brothers, and to conform to the intentions of nature, there must be classes of citizens who are more highly esteemed than others ; but no man should be stigmatized by, and humiliated in, his condition. . . . In spite of the distinctions attached to the different orders of the state, they should be equal among themselves so far as they can be at the present time ; they will neither despise nor oppress each other, if the

[1] XII, 93.   [2] XVII, 116 seq.   [3] XVIII, 340.

law has taken wise precautions to balance their powers and to make the particular rights of each sacred and inviolable." [1]

On this formal basis material measures can then be built up. In the first place stands logically the repression of incommensurate riches in its most striking manifestation, incommensurate display : " It is easy to make sumptuary laws which would diminish our greed by making wealth less necessary." But we must not stop at the symptoms. Besides the most striking demonstrations of incommensurate wealth its most important actual form, the *latifundium*, must be fought : " It is even easy to make agrarian laws which prevent avarice from swallowing up all possessions and which, little by little, bring about the disappearance of those scandalous fortunes which are an eternal source of injustice, vexation, tyranny, and servitude." [2] Landed property is, however, only an incarnation (if the most repulsive one) of incommensurate property. In order really to fulfil its mission the state must take measures directed at reducing differences of possession of all kinds. In the solution of this problem Mably actually resorted to the expedient Raynal had advocated : the reform of the law of inheritance.

" In a well-governed state the legislator would undoubtedly introduce formalities which would impede the sale and alienation of goods. In order to preserve greater equality in fortune he would undoubtedly not allow of the last will. The law would dispose of the possessions of all deceased persons. . . . Lay down what degrees of relationship give a right to a share in a vacant inheritance ; but do not extend these too far, lest too wide hopes should open the soul to prodigality and avarice. The only daughter of a citizen would bring a dangerous fortune into her husband's family. . . . So she should possess only the third part of the estate, and her father or her guardians should give her two adopted brothers. If a man has no heir, his wealth should not belong to the state, which ought to give an example of disinterestedness ; the inheritance should be equally divided among the poor families of the district which he who left it had inhabited. How fortunate would it be if the rich grew accustomed to regard the needy as their sons, their brothers and their heirs. . . . I say in a word that good legislation should continually break up and divide the fortunes which avarice and ambition continually labour to amass." [3]

By such means it is possible to fight social inequality. But

[1] XVIII, 339. [2] XVIII, 340. [3] XII, 135 seq.

it is impossible to reconstitute social equality. Hence it follows that the existence of social classes must be taken as the starting-point of a realistic theory and policy. However—paradoxical though it may sound—even the contrast of classes, rightly handled, may become a means of lessening the tensions in society and strengthening social peace : namely when it is possible to balance the antagonistic elements so that they mutually check each other. Mably, who regarded the state of free play of equal individual forces as an unattainable ideal, conceived the state of free equilibrium of equal class forces as the best possible order of society. To achieve this state is his practical programme ; this state is the standard by which he judges the phenomena of reality.

This theory of free equilibrium of class forces is only a special case of the theory of free equilibrium of political forces which in the eighteenth century was common in international, and national English, politics. It was the thought of others which Mably expressed when he put forward the demand that the political power should be divided : " To ask which is the best government, monarchy, aristocracy, or democracy, is like asking what greater or lesser evils the passions of a prince, of a senate, or those of the multitude may produce." [1] In their full purity all three forms are bad : even Raynal had said in this sense [2] that absolute monarchy was tyranny, democracy tended towards anarchy, and aristocracy, oscillating between these two poles, realized the faults of both. Mably, however, believed the problem to have been already solved in the philosophy of antiquity. For Plato " censured monarchy, pure aristocracy, and popular government. Never, he said, are the laws in safety under those administrations which leave too free a course to the passions. He feared the power of a prince who, being the only legislator, was sole judge of the justice of his laws. He was afraid, in aristocracy, of the pride and avarice of the great who, in the belief that all was owed to them, would without scruple sacrifice the interest of society to their particular advantage. He dreaded in pure democracy the caprices of the multitude, who are always blind, always extreme in their demands, and will passionately condemn to-morrow what they enthusiastically approve today. This great man . . . desired that, by a clever mixture of all these forms of government, the public power should be divided into different parts proper to limit, balance and mitigate each other." [3]

[1] XIV, 79. [2] *Op. cit.* VIII, 57. [3] XIV, 78–80.

This was Mably's programme also. In classical Sparta he believed he saw it realized : " The republic of Lycurgus, uniting all the advantages of which aristocracy, royalty, and democracy can possess only a small part, if they are not combined to form a single government, had none of the vices which are natural to them. The sovereignty which the people enjoyed carried them without effort to all those great and magnanimous deeds which the love of liberty and the fatherland may produce in a purely popular state. As soon as the democratic part of the government wished to abuse their authority, they found themselves without sufficient strength to do so, and limited by the influence of the magistrates, in consequence of the equilibrium established between the different powers. . . . In consequence of the same equilibrium of powers, the magistrates, who were in their turn almighty if the law marched behind them, found themselves under the imperious hand of the people as soon as they deviated from this rule. . . . Great abuses were impossible." [1] But unlike Lycurgus, unlike Plato, and indeed even unlike Locke, Mably sought to found the equilibrium of political powers on, and secure it by, an equilibrium of social forces.

" In a country where men are distributed among different orders, and where consequently they enjoy varying degrees of wealth and consideration, I feel that it is impossible to impose the same rules upon avarice and ambition as under a democratic government ; but even if it is not possible to attain to perfection, should we neglect to approach towards it ? Why should not a certain patrimony be established for each order ? In Sweden we have a beginning of this custom ; there are estates which can be possessed only by gentlemen, and others only by burghers. . . . Why is there no distinction between noblemen's lands, church lands, and lands of commoners, which according to their distribution could be owned only by noblemen, ecclesiastics or commoners ? If the fortune of every citizen could change, diminish, or grow, within his class, at least the fortune of every order would remain the same and none would fall into disdain." [2]

This, then, is the constitution of state and society at which, according to Mably, all nations should aim. It was in his mind when he wrote his *Observations sur le Gouvernement et les Lois des États-unis d'Amérique*. This last of his works showed even more clearly than all the others the most conspicuous trait of his

[1] V, 19 seq.   [2] XII, 139 seq.

character, which naturally in his old age became still more predominant: his scepticism and pessimism, which turned the philanthropist Mably into a misanthrope.

It is not surprising to find that Mably did not reproach the United States with the fact of slavery. Bondage is everywhere, inequality is everywhere, and in the North as in the South of the Union the same system prevails: " All your constitutions ", he says, " have taken into their protection, all those, who, because they have not contributed to the expences of the public, and have sold to masters the labour of their hands, are not yet members of the Republic. These Men, who under the description of slaves, were despised by the ancients, and who, even in Europe, with the title of free-men languish in real servitude, you have had the address to attach to the fate of the republic by affording them the means of rising superior to their station, of acquiring a peculium, and cultivating an industry that will raise them to the rank of citizens." [1]

It is characteristic of Mably that he hardly distinguished here between slaves and wage-earners, black men and white. He who does not possess anything but the strength of his arms and is forced to sell it, is, in his eyes, a slave. It is likely indeed that by this word he described exclusively, or at least predominantly, the class which we call the proletariat. " It seems that the author does not allude here to the negroes," Mazzei held.[2] " The law has not opened to them a way to the rights of citizenship, nor furnished them with the means of acquiring a peculium so that they might rise above their station." But Mably saw no difference.

Certainly, in America the human laws which admit of slavery violate the laws of nature which have ordained that all men shall be equal. " But are not these sacred laws violated in the states where some citizens possess all and others have nothing ? I beg to remark that the liberty which every European believes himself to enjoy is nothing but the possibility of breaking his chain in order to give himself up to a new master. Want here makes the slaves ; and they are the more miserable, since no law provides for their subsistence. It is mendicancy that degrades man ; and this is inevitable with all nations that have not imposed limitations upon the cupidity and fortunes of

---

[1] Engl. trans., *Observations on the Government and Laws of the United States of America*, London 1784, 9 seq.
[2] *Recherches historiques et politiques sur les États-Unis de l'Amérique Septentrionale*, 1788, II, 17 seq.

citizens. . . . It is mockery of reason to pretend that all men are free in the countries where one citizen employs the other to serve him and condemns him to employments most low and most hard for humanity." [1]

Hence America is, in spite of her inegalitarian social constitution, no worse than the rest of the world. But neither is she better, in spite of her egalitarian political constitution. " Can anyone, without some degree of apprehension, consider the vast variety of individuals of whom every community consists, all endued with active, and yet each with different, passions? Of these, however, some are incapable of reflection, and this class consists of by far the greatest number : others are able only to combine the ideas that are proposed to them ; and amidst these, a few men of genius distinguish themselves, who will not always, however, be of the same sentiments. What then must become of a republic [the Republic of North America] if it has not in itself a body permanently established, that shall religiously preserve the deposit of the national laws, policy, and character, as the Vestals preserved the sacred fire of Vesta ? Let us, Sir, analyse the histories of Lacedemon and Rome, and you will plainly perceive that these two republics were indebted for all their virtue, their policy, their wisdom, their fortitude, and in short for that character which we so much admire, to no other cause than the establishment of that perpetual senate which was the soul of the State. By this the Aristocracy and Democracy were held in exact equilibrium ; and hence resulted a mixed form of government, which preserved the advantages of each mode, without having the defects of either." [2]

Thus the ancient republics of Europe rested on the principle of the equilibrium of class forces ; the modern republics of America, however, rest on the equilibrium of individual forces. This experiment cannot succeed, ideal though its conception may be. Indeed, it seemed certain to Mably that the striving of the new state after the highest harmony, because it followed the wrong track, must and would lead to the greatest disharmony. " I will agree with you," he addresses John Adams, " that a Democracy ought to be the basis of every government . . . The people in this mode of government alone, can interest themselves in the welfare of their country. . . . But you will, I believe, acknowledge with me, that a Democracy must be managed, tempered, and established, with the utmost prudence. You will

[1] IX, 258 seq. [2] *Observations,* 35 seq.

observe that the multitude, degraded by their necessities, and by employments which condemn them to ignorance, and to mean and sordid sentiments, have neither opportunity nor time to acquire the liberal principles of a wise policy. Influenced by their prejudices, they will judge of the welfare of the state, according to their particular interests, and whatever most promotes these, they will deem the wisest measures. The people cannot believe themselves free without being tempted to abuse their liberty, because they have passions, which are constantly endeavouring to throw off every restraint. . . . They will naturally envy the lot of their superiors, and wish either to rise to an equality with them, or to degrade them to their own level. What are the consequences of this? The citizens of the first class have also their passions, which take fire at the pretended insolence of the people. . . . Minds are inflamed ; one act of injustice renders another necessary ; reproaches arise ; revenge alone then usurps the place of policy ; Revolutions succeed each other. . . ."[1] In a word, the very formal equality of rights must bring forth the opposition of classes if the germ of such an opposition is contained in the conditions.

In the American conditions the germ of such an opposition of classes undoubtedly is contained : the class contrast between nobility and commoners which—leading by way of the contrast between rich and poor—will end in the class contrast between possessors and dispossessed. " In consequence of your former connections with England, you have among you the seeds of an aristocracy, which will continually increase in growth. . . . Your principal care should then have been to set limits to the Aristocracy, and to make laws, that might restrain the rich from abusing their wealth, and from purchasing an authority which ought not to belong to them." But instead of acknowledging the fact of class division and rendering it harmless by a wise social policy, the attempt has been undertaken to organize society on the basis of a fictitious equality. No good can be expected of this experiment. " I fear that the rich will endeavour to form a separate order, and to seize upon the whole authority ; in this, others, proud of the equality with which they have been flattered, will refuse to acquiesce ; and hence will necessarily result the dissolution of the government you designed to establish. . . . Hence I foresee hatred, jealousy, passions which know no limits in their career, and which lead on in their train a thousand other

[1] 11–13.

vices, the harbingers of a tyranny fluctuating between rashness and timidity." [1]

The nearer a colony's political constitution seems to approach to the principle of equality, the worse it is in Mably's view. Therefore he casts the darkest horoscope for the commonwealth of the Quakers : " All the United States of America have required a certain quantity of property both in representatives, and Electors : *Pensylvania* alone admits to these privileges, all inhabitants, without exception, who have, during a year, contributed towards the support of government. It appears from this arrangement, that the Legislator has paid a greater attention to merit than to fortune ; and, on the first view, nothing can seem more strictly just. But may there not be some circumstances, Sir, in which the greatest good being unattainable, it is most prudent to be satisfied with a less perfect establishment? If a republic is so fortunate as to be yet unacquainted with either riches or poverty, this law of Pensylvania may, and ought to be enacted, because, without being contradictory to the public manners, it will be favourable to the Democracy. But if fortune has already made such a difference in the circumstances of the citizens, as to render a distinction of rank unavoidable ; instead of endeavouring after a pure Democracy, would it not be more prudent to grant to the people only such privileges and rights, as are necessary to render the Aristocracy more circumspect, and prevent it from indulging that ambition, to which it is naturally prone ? " Without social equality even political liberty is problematic : " Who can be certain that no wealthy merchant by affecting popular politics, shall take advantage of those discontents, hatreds, and jealousies, which are continually springing up in a Democracy where property is so unequally distributed, to kindle the flames of evil discord, to make trial of his power, and to establish his tyranny ? " [2] At the moment it may perhaps seem as if equality and democracy were founded in, and safeguarded by, the conditions. But the evil is already within the walls : " I have been informed that the Pensylvanians apply much more to agriculture than to commerce, and that those enormous and disproportionate fortunes, which are but too frequently found in the republic of Massachusets are unknown among them. This may be true ; but is this sufficient to vindicate their Democracy ? I know that agriculture produces greater simplicity and purity of manners than commerce ; but I observe

[1] 16 seq., 18 seq.   [2] 23, 25 seq.

that the Port of Philadelphia affords a favourable avenue to trade and industry. If the Pensylvanians take a delight in riches produced from their lands, why should they neglect increasing this wealth by following the example of the Bostonians ? I ask what measures the laws have taken to stop them on the brink of their precipice ? I ask farther, if, in a government entirely popular, any such measures can be taken ? When a people industriously cultivate the earth, in order to enrich themselves, and must soon have shops and mechanics to work and fashion raw materials to assist and expedite the progress even of agriculture ; it would be a miracle of the most extraordinary kind, if they were able to resist the farther impulse of a sentiment, by which they cannot but be actuated . . . and in this case, I once more ask, what are the resources of a Democracy ? " [1]

While Mably thus regards as most unfavourable the prospects of the state which most closely approached to equality, his prognosis is best for that member of the union which is farthest from it : " Perhaps, Sir, you may have the mortification to see Pensylvania a prey to all the humours of a Democracy, while the government of *Massachusets* will be confirmed in its principles." The constitution of this state is more reminiscent of the principles of an aristocracy than of those of popular government. For " the plan of government established in Massachusets is formed after the model of that of England." Mably means by this : Massachusetts is consciously organized as a class state. The difference from the mother-country is merely that it is not the bourgeoisie that is subject to the nobles, but the proletariat to the bourgeoisie. " I observe, Sir, with pleasure ", says Mably the misanthrope and pessimist, " that the government keeps at a proper distance all those who have no property but their labour, and who could only disturb the political administration, were any authority allowed to them." The interests of the poor are sufficiently protected, if a possibility of economic ascent is granted them. Moreover, care has been taken that the rich cannot abuse their power, and that is all that can possibly be desired. " By rendering the possession of less property necessary to qualify for representative, than for senator, you have, by a prudent equilibrium, prevented the more wealthy citizens from engrossing among themselves the whole authority. This is, in my opinion, the most proper arrangement that could be made to moderate the Aristocracy, by mixing something of democracy with it." [2]

[1] 42.   [2] 39, 37, 43.

How great is the contrast between this sober praise and the high ideal that Mably bore in his heart! Only once does it come to the surface in this most sombre of all his writings, and this passage is like a fine lyric in a naturalistic novel: the warm words devoted to the then young republic of *Georgia*.[1] " Friends, Brethren," he addresses in his mind the constituent assembly of this state, " let us return thanks to Providence for having directed America to the happy revolution that secures its independence, previous to that period, when from our increased populousness and wealth, it might perhaps be impossible for us to secure our liberties on a permanent basis." Populousness creates a proletariat, wealth a class of capitalists, and the foundations of social harmony are destroyed. Georgia has not yet gone so far: " We are not now so numerous as to prevent our conferring, and our manners, yet uncorrupted by artificial wants, still permit us to establish in our infant republic the true principles of society, and to erect barriers that shall exclude those vices, which either permit not men to take the path that leads to happiness, or make them soon abandon it. The only true wealth of man is the produce of the earth; would we be really happy, let us learn to be contented with the fruit which we reap from our labour; this will always suffice, and will never fail us. . . . Would to God, no ship might ever arrive, which, by importing pleasures and wants hitherto unknown, would render us disgusted with a simplicity that is sufficient for our happiness. . . . Let us avoid following the example of Europe, wretched from the attempt to found her strength, her power, and her happiness upon a wealth that must weaken and impoverish her. From the moment that we look upon commerce as the object and end of a flourishing State, we must renounce all the principles of sound policy. . . ."

However sincerely these words may be meant and felt, they were not spoken for all America. The arch-evils of inequality, ambition and avarice, seemed to Mably already too deeply rooted in the hearts of the Americans. He was firmly convinced that the New World would go the way of the Old—a way which, beginning with the introduction of private property, could not but end in disaster.

" Permit me, Sir, . . . to trace, step by step, the progress of those evils, which I apprehend for the United States of America. At first, and as long as your principal cities seek only to extend and multiply their connections and business, the republic will

[1] 45-7.

appear tranquil and flourishing. . . . The cultivators in the country will as yet perceive only the advantages of commerce : the produce of the earth will acquire a new value : Encouraged by the profits of agriculture, the labourer will clear uncultivated lands, population will increase, because children are no burden to their parents ; and at the same time, manufactures will be established in every place, which will be equally serviceable in promoting commerce and agriculture. As yet, this picture presents nothing formidable to those who are not accustomed to peruse the page of futurity." As yet there is an equality, at least of opportunities, which secures a social harmony. " But let us examine the infant and growing vices, which are concealed under these flattering appearances. A spirit of commerce will, in my opinion, soon become the general and predominant spirit of the inhabitants of your cities. Those, who do not entirely resign themselves to its influence, must submit to comparative poverty, and sink themselves beneath the level of those traders, whose wealth is daily increasing. I believe, that those, who are thus newly enriched, will at first have only that gross and foolish vanity, which wealth inspires. Without despising those citizens who have been less fortunate, they will only deem their own abilities greater. . . . But after the second, or, at furthest, the third generation, do you imagine that their children, born in the midst of wealth, will not have the passions, which it infallibly inspires ? With what eye then will they behold that equality, which your laws were intended to establish among citizens ? They will have no ideas of those inalienable rights of sovereignty, which you have ascribed to the people. As among all nations, whether ancient or modern, riches have been the source and principle of that nobility, of which men are so vain ; what miraculous circumstance shall prevent their dividing families in America into different classes ? Wealth establishes the most essential and sensible difference between man and man ; whence then can you expect, that, among you, it will suffer the poor to enjoy equal advantages with the rich ? Your constitution must therefore necessarily undergo a dissolution." [1]

A war of classes will be the consequence. It could be avoided only if men would overcome the attractions of wealth : " I foresee perpetual contests, between that Aristocracy, which the passions will establish, and that Democracy, which the laws will protect ; and to prevent this from being disadvantageous, and

[1] 91–3.

even ruinous to the republic, the citizens must possess the virtues of the best ages of Rome ; that is, there must be something which, in their esteem, is more precious than wealth." [1] Will the inhabitants of America reach this moral height ? Mably the pessimist—or should we not say Mably the realist ?—answers No. Therefore an attempt to mitigate the threatening evils that simply cannot be avoided, is the only measure that can reasonably be undertaken. " With the manners we have in Europe, and which probably are already too general in America, wealth must at last usurp an absolute empire. All efforts made to oppose it will be fruitless ; but it is not impossible, by many precautions, to prevent this empire from becoming tyrannical." [2] The first step on this path is the suppression of all demonstrative expressions of the class contrast : " Sumptuary laws, and regulations favourable to purity of manners must prevent the progress of luxury, and diminish the artificial wants of effeminacy and vanity, passions that know no limits, that in time ruin even monarchies, but are immediate destruction to republics. It is by such public and general discipline that the education of your children will be truly compleated." [3] But measures of this sort do not suffice : the problem of society, the conflict of classes, is too keen.

" You may be assured, Sir, that your people, whose supremacy the laws have so evidently established, will be difficult to manage, because they will feel their power. . . . They will be uneasy and suspicious, from seeing that some of their fellow-citizens, who are not at all superior to them in point of rights, are nevertheless so proud of their fortune, as to refuse to mix with them, and affect a certain superiority. This is an incurable disorder, incident to all free states in which property is very unequally divided. . . . What is then the regimen best suited to such a constitution ? This will in my opinion consist of conciliatory laws, which, without depriving the poor of any of their rights, will prevent the rich from the abuse of those passions, which their wealth inspires. The people derive from the mediocrity of their fortunes a kind of moderation, from which, unless irritated by contempt or injustice, they seldom depart. Wealth, on the contrary, inspires its possessors with a vanity, which is the more insolent, as it is void of reason. It wishes to govern, and assumes the wish as a privilege. . . . Why tend not the laws to divide those fortunes, which the avarice of the wealthy would accumulate without end ? Why do they not, by marking

[1] 30.   [2] 120.   [3] 53.

luxury with contempt, deprive rapacity of the aliment that feeds, and renders it insatiable? Had the American constitutions been established upon these principles, I should have observed with pleasure, that you were aware of the danger to which your republics are exposed, and had, at least, endeavoured to establish in the state a bond of peace and concord, and to fix liberty on a firm and lasting basis." [1] This has not been done. Now, the legislators can hardly do more than save their good name : " If you take proper measures to prevent commerce from multiplying your wants ; if you oppose the progress of luxury, if your laws are prudently diffident of women, by whom corruption has been introduced into every republic, if you set bounds to the ambition of the rich, who are naturally inclined to think that every thing is their due, because possessed of that wealth, to which every thing submits ; in a word, if you endeavour to establish among all your citizens . . . such an equilibrium, as leaves reason to conclude that you have exerted every possible effort to fix liberty firmly on the basis of laws, you need not fear that the evils, with which America may at any time be afflicted, will be imputed to you. . . . But however this may be, Sir ; it is beyond a doubt, that as soon as your republics are enriched by an extensive commerce, their citizens will assume the genius and character peculiar to traders. . . . This prospect of prodigious wealth makes me tremble for the lot that awaits you. . . . Every bale of merchandize, imported or exported, will certainly become, like Pandora's box, a source of evils to the republic." [2]

Only one counsel can Mably offer to the young commonwealth, and that is not very hopeful : to make the central power as strong as possible, because it is somewhat removed from the social disputes in the individual states. " I can see only one resource for the Americans, which is, to render the continental Congress the supreme judge of every difference that may arise between the several ranks of citizens, in all the states of the union. . . . If the rich should oppose the law I have suggested, it would be a certain sign that they already form projects either of vanity or of ambition. This I cannot think, Sir ; and I rather hope, that if they are convinced my apprehensions are not chimerical, they will with pleasure behold a power established in your confederacy, that is favorable to equality, that will preserve the first class of citizens from an ambition, which would terminate in their ruin, and the lowest ranks from a servility or

[1] 75-7. [2] 98 seq., 84 seq.

wretchedness, the effects of which, notwithstanding all their endeavours to avoid it, would soon recoil upon the wealthy."[1] In this way the American ideal cannot, indeed, be preserved, but its decline will at least be quiet and painless :

"Then, Sir, if, as I have too much reason to fear, the American confederacy should by its commerce and manners be inclined or impelled towards Aristocracy, the transition will be imperceptible, without violence, or commotion. The claims of the rich will be gradually allowed, but the rights of the poor will still be protected. Custom will establish expedients to which it is impossible to give the sanction of laws ; but which habit will render tolerable, and at length sacred. The Poor, not being oppressed, will be reconciled by custom to their lot ; subordination will be no longer offensive to the people, who, as they are happy, will conclude that the distinctions enjoyed by the rich are legally their due. Thus an Aristocracy, enjoying its prerogatives in peace, will . . . be free from the vices natural to it."[2] This slow transition to a stable state of classes seems to Mably the best that can be hoped for the United States of America.

[1] 113 seq.   [2] 116 seq.

CHAPTER IV

CHASTELLUX THE CRITIC

In contrast to Gabriel Bonnot de Mably, François-Jean de Chastellux was no *laudator temporis acti*. The two men had, in long discussions, contended about the problem of the greatest happiness of the greatest number without reaching an agreement. While Mably was convinced that the lot of mankind had steadily deteriorated in the course of the centuries, Chastellux confidently believed in a steady progress towards perfect society. In his main work, *De la Félicité Publique, ou Considérations sur le sort des hommes dans les différentes époques de l'histoire* (1772), which was intended as a counterstroke to Mably's *Entretiens de Phocion*, Chastellux's philosophy of history is stated clearly in the following words: " If I may be permitted to judge according to my own impressions I shall not disavow the inward sentiment which makes me love the age in which I have begun my career and to which the study of history always leads me back with the same feeling of pleasure which is experienced by a traveller who, after having wandered through savage countries, at last finds himself again in his native land." [1]

It is obvious what practical conclusion must be drawn from this theoretical attitude: the conclusion that a reconstruction of society, whether in the form of a revolution or of a radical reformation, must be rejected. For " good itself may sometimes be bought at too high a price. London is more regular than Paris, Dieppe than Rouen, Mannheim than Strasbourg; but London, Dieppe, and Mannheim have all at some time been consumed by the flames. What architect would ever advise setting fire to Paris in order to rebuild it afterwards according to a regular and magnificent plan? " [2]

Chastellux here shows himself to be a genuine aristocrat of the *Ancien Régime*. But he was an enlightened aristocrat. He did not deny the evils in society, but he believed that time itself would heal them: " I will not say all is well, but all is better. There is progress; there is ground for hope." [3] But precisely to prevent these hopes from being nipped in the bud, precisely to ensure that this progress should unfold its blessings, it was

[1] Ed. of 1776, reprint of 1822, II, 95 seq.   [2] II, 114.   [3] II, 113.

necessary to protect society from great convulsions. This is the true interest of all social orders, and especially of the lower classes : " The greatest good fortune that any nation can have is to preserve its princes and its government. The progress of reason should tend to perfection rather than to change." [1]

This conservatism was in opposition not only to the opinions of Mably and Raynal, but generally to the dominant sentiment of the time. Had not rationalism taught for a hundred years that there is a best state which the mind can and must conceive by pure contemplation, and politics realize through radical change ? Had not the philosophers proved that men must not passively wait for the order of reason to come into being, but must actively create it ? Chastellux did not fail to grasp the force of this doctrine. But he was courageous enough to contrast it with a perfect counter-doctrine.

To the dogmatic absolutism of the rationalists Chastellux, anticipating the nineteenth century, opposed the historical relativism of empiricism. He was convinced that social science —the science of social felicity—would be led astray by *à priori* suppositions : " In the study of morals as in that of nature one must assume as little as possible." [2] Thus, approaching without prejudice the investigation of the great question of human coexistence, one is led to the conclusion that there is no eternal answer, and everything depends upon circumstances : " It is merely frivolous and useless to raise such questions as : Are men in a state of perpetual war against each other ? Are they born friends or enemies of one another ? . . . They are friends when, lending each other mutual support, they can more easily satisfy their needs : they are enemies if circumstances establish competition between them, if several wish to obtain what only one can enjoy. Savage fishers should be more united among themselves than savage hunters ; the nomadic nations more than either." [3]

From this point of view all discussion of a prehistoric state of nature appears senseless : " Let us distrust these sublime dreams . . . and content ourselves with the assurance that the state of society has effaced the last traces of what one calls the state of nature. In fact, what are civilized men ? Whether they have deteriorated or become perfected, they are totally new beings. . . ." [4]

Once society has developed, even the most fundamental

[1] II, 91.   [2] II, 242.   [3] I, 22.   [4] I, 23.

instincts of nature submit to its moulding influence. What stronger natural instinct can there be than the love of the sexes and the love of children? And yet they appear in different social classes in different forms: "Whatever profession a man has chosen, whatever work he is engaged on, he must have a wife: but often the necessity of our living stands in contradiction to this other, no less imperative, necessity; we must seek to reconcile them. The factory worker, the day labourer, the domestic servant, the soldier cannot live with their families; they take a wife without taking a companion; and still they can only gain this wife by binding themselves to her by stricter and more durable bonds than those by which the sweetest custom could ever unite us. The wife herself, alone charged with the care of the household, does not follow this command of nature any better. Maternal tenderness must be silent before the voice of interest." [1]

Nothing would be more senseless, nothing more impossible than to force upon society in the developed state a primitive law of nature. Indeed, what is the law of nature? What is the state of nature? What else can it be but that state in which man has not as yet overcome his animal origin? To the fanciful eighteenth-century opinion which believed in a prehistoric golden age, Chastellux opposed the sober view of the nineteenth century that man has descended from the ape. Therefore not many words need be wasted on primeval man: "It will suffice . . . to observe that savage man, brute man, very near to the animal, leads us firmly to believe that his particular character comprises nothing contrary to the plan which nature seems to have followed with regard to all living creatures. . . . To subsist and to reproduce themselves: that is the general law which she has imposed upon them; and this simple law is carried out by means as simple as itself. Pleasure and pain are the only ministers that second it: pleasure attached to all the means of preservation and multiplication; pain annexed to all the means of destruction. Starting from this principle, which it is impossible to d   it is not difficult to see that the happiness of all that exist   sists solely in fulfilling the wish of nature. The individual th   s developed, has subsisted, and has reproduced itself to the a. which has been assigned to it, will certainly have enjoyed the happiness of which it is capable, since pleasure   ill have duly accompanied the functions useful to its life." [2]

[1] I, 24.   [2] II, 237 seq.

In this primitive state social equality and social harmony in fact prevail (if it is at all possible to speak of social relations) : " To all . . . the advantages which beings enjoy under the hands of nature we must add also the uniformity of situation between individuals of the same species. We know indeed that there are animals which thrive better in a certain country and under certain circumstances ; but wherever they prosper, they all prosper alike ; wherever they suffer, they all suffer alike : hence no reproaches, no humiliating and painful comparisons ; . . . and . . . from this point of view, the happiness of the individual cannot be different from that of the species." [1]

But this equality and harmony are due only to animal nature : the identity of the individuals is the greater, the lower the species stands in its development : " The less complicated is the organization of creatures, the more similar are their actions. The nests of the birds, the holes of the rabbits, the hives of the bees are commonly similar to each other. The same must be true of manners ; founded on the needs common to all, they are the same for all individuals of the same species." [2]

As long as men are no more than half-apes equality, indeed, prevails among them—but only so long and no longer. " We need not doubt that the same observations are applicable to men truly savage and brute ; but let us state at the same time that it is very difficult to find the human race in that primitive state, which I shall not call the state of nature, because I am convinced that it is in the nature of man to perfect his faculties, as it is in the nature of a child to become a grown man . . . Men do not remain in that humiliating state . . . and it is only the progress of the perfected species which we have to consider, if we wish to appreciate the happiness of which they are capable." [3]

For— and this raises man above the animal—nature has endowed the human race with the possibility of boundless perfection, and this perfection necessarily called forth differences of development : " Considering man only physically, we find that the sense of touch and the perfectibility of language have furnished him with such advantages over all other animals that his organization, growing more and more perfect every day, has in the end become too complex not to be varied and too subtle not to be irregular." [4]

In this way the higher development of the human race brings forth the problems of human society : " The first reflexion which

[1] II, 38 seq.   [2] I, 19 seq.   [3] II, 239 seq.   [4] I, 20.

presents itself to our mind is this : Since the human species is the most perfectible of all, and could not exercise this faculty in an equal and uniform manner, the result has necessarily been a great inequality in the fate of individuals. One nation, better assisted by the climate, by the fertility of the soil, by the resources which it may have found in rich hunting grounds and fishing waters, will have become enlightened earlier than its neighbours : in this nation some men will have made a more useful application of the knowledge thus acquired ; they will have perfected and enlarged it : but what use can man make of his industry and his strength, if it is not to augment his power, to multiply his enjoyments or to obtain them more easily ? The first arms were perhaps destined for making war on animals ; but men did not hesitate to use them against their fellows. Courage is only the awareness of our own strength : hence the inequality of forces necessarily favoured [the rise of] violence, and violence, in the end, gave birth to war." [1]

Ascent, for good or ill, is the fate of man : it brought evil into the world, and by it the evil will be conquered. " The state of war has become man's habitual state. It was necessary either to inspire terror or to resent it ; to be either oppressor or oppressed. But in the moral world that has happened which happens quite frequently in the physical world. From the very excess of evil has sprung its remedy. The necessity of combining, whether for attack or defence, has formed or strengthened the ties of society and given rise to government and legislation. . . . Attack and defence were the object of the first associations, and internal and external pacification that of the first laws. . . . I say that war alone, force and violence, have called forth all that still exists among us : thus all constitutions, even those which are in power in our days, are to my mind only peace treaties." [2]

But even if the union of men in social bodies has—at least to a certain extent—overcome the war of all against all, it has not reconstituted social harmony : " From the organization of society, however, even from the introduction of government, have sprung different relations of inequality among men : inequality in the fate of different nations, inequality of fortune and condition among men subject to the same laws. . . . What then is the remedy for this misfortune of the human race ? If you wish to find it, remember the origin of the evil : men are capable of perfection, and that in the highest degree ; but the greatest

[1] II, 240 seq.   [2] II, 242, 285.

inequality prevails in their progress, and it will only be at the consummation of this progress that they will be able to meet. Let us therefore try to accelerate its course, to make the way smooth for all; and far from founding the happiness [of an individual or] of a nation on pre-eminence . . . over others, do not claim more than your part in the felicity of all: happy is the division where, as by magic, each part increases in the proportion in which it is subdivided; where men become richer by what they give away; where happiness is the lot of all."[1]

Chastellux here approaches for one moment the ideal of his time. But he sees it only at a nebulous distance, at the end of history, as the product of the highest perfection of men. It is impossible to create this state artificially: " Nothing is more frivolous than all the efforts to find the best form of government of which men are capable. It would not be sufficient to have found it; to realize it, it would be necessary to control all the circumstances; to form a state according to one's fancy it would be necessary to be master of the whole world. What am I saying? Still more would be necessary: it would be necessary to extend one's empire over times past, to efface memory and habit; in a word to destroy and to create everything."[2]

It is not given to man to accomplish this superhuman work of destruction and new creation. Chastellux has nothing but scorn for the schemers of Mably's kind: " Here ", he says of the world improvers, " to make men happy, they wish to reduce them to the state of the brute; that is to say, to keep a ball in repose, they place it at the top of an inclined plane which it must always of necessity descend: there, they suggest banishing commerce and industry, because luxury follows at their heels: elsewhere they forbid men to reason, lest they should differ in their opinions; one man alone, or perhaps a class of men, is charged with thinking on behalf of a whole nation. However, what has happened so far? The rapid current has swept away the man who, guiding his ship . . . tried in vain to resist its force, but the latter has arrived at the safe port, while the former was smashed against the mast. Lycurgus, in his republic, wanted only iron money: what was the result? That the Persians needed less gold to corrupt the generals of Lacedæmon. The Roman Senate insisted on giving only two acres of land to each citizen: what was the outcome of this rigour? That the first tribune to order the distribution of double the amount overthrew

[1] II, 243 seq.   [2] II, 272.

the constitution. In modern times the Inquisition prosecutes Galileo : and the useful knowledge passes to the islanders who soon become the most powerful enemies of the pontiffs. Well ! Let things take their course according to their natural trend ; and since man is capable of perfection, we may be certain that he will not rest until he has reached the highest degree of science and industry to which he might aspire." [1]

Indeed, this conviction is the reconciling element in Chastellux's social philosophy. Ideal society cannot be realized by artificial means, but it realizes itself in a natural way. The individual spontaneously follows the right track, and the state can follow it consciously : " In all conditions there is an irresistible attraction leading all beings towards the best possible state, and it is here that we have to seek the natural revelation which should serve as oracle to all legislators." [2]

In all the variety of the world this great teleology is at work. " All nations cannot have the same government ; in one nation all cities, all classes of citizens cannot have the same laws, the same administration, and the same customs ; but all generally can strive after the greatest possible happiness." [3]

In so far as all men aim at this one absolute goal, there is also one absolute rule for their actions. But it consists in the end only in confiding in the theodicy : " There are undoubtedly fundamental principles which concern all nations and all legal systems ; but it seems that they are negative rather than positive ; that is to say they reveal what should not, rather than what should be done."

If the world can go on its way without interference, all will be for the best : " Remember that you govern beings capable of perfection," Chastellux addresses the powerful of the earth. " Let them therefore advance in the way of reason ! Do not arrest or direct their progress ; but do not cease to keep an eye on this progress, to follow it on its way, and incessantly to adapt yourselves to it ; progress will be the surest guide to truth, and it is in truth that you must find the only foundation of all legislation and the principle of all government." [4]

But just because universal history is the universal road from suffering to joy and from evil to happiness, man at present cannot be quite happy. For in the present the bitter aftertaste of the past is mixed with the sweet foretaste of the future : " This is the great obstacle to public felicity, that all that is partakes of

[1] II, 245 seq.   [2] I, 26.   [3] I, 27.   [4] II, 271.

what has been. . . . Hence the public evils spring much less from present than from past errors, and it is unjust to mistrust human reason, the progress of which would have a more rapid effect if it had not to combat prejudice and customs, all of which arose and were formed in the times of ignorance." [1]

Peaceful progress is the remedy for all evils. "Wherever we turn our eyes, we see only one great course on the surface of the globe where some run rapidly and the others drag painfully along, hurt and trodden down by those who seek to overtake them ; and we shall be led to the reflection that, even if the disproportion in the fates of individuals is an inconvenience necessarily attached to the perfectibility of the human race, the safest remedy of this inconvenience is yet the greatest acceleration in the march of progress." [2]

Peaceful progress comprises all parts of society. "If a nation perfects itself by the natural progress of enlightenment, it improves at the same time all the factors that lead to general prosperity : legislation, commerce, agriculture, military affairs, navigation, all march in step ; and then happiness is founded on a broad and durable basis." [3]

Is it not obvious how progress widens the happiness in society ? Is it not obvious how it brings happiness even to the unsuccessful who are being outstripped only for a limited time by their more dynamic competitors? "Experience is the best and perhaps the only instrument of instruction. . . . Commerce existed long before the science of commerce, and it was then very remunerative. Finance arose and expanded long before its details and principles were known. The veil begins to be lifted and at once profits are limited, except in new ventures." [4] It cannot be doubted that the progress of some, in the end, leads to the progress of all. Hence *sub specie æternitatis* inequality is good, because it is born of progress and gives birth to progress, which, in its turn, promotes equality. But what is the result if we consider it *sub specie temporis* ?

"This point alone could give a great advantage to the detractors of society. . . . What ! they will say to me, you pity a horde of savages because they live in hovels and have no clothing other than the skins of animals : behold, in the streets of your proud cities, behold a miserable wretch covered with rags who with effort carries a painful burden while his fellow, rapidly riding by in a magnificent carriage, robs him of the very

[1] II, 275, 277.   [2] II, 247 seq.   [3] II, 227.   [4] II, 247.

use of the roadway and adds danger to his labours. . . . It is not given to men to judge otherwise than by comparison, and it is only on seeing men more fortunate than ourselves that we feel unhappy." [1]

Chastellux believes even this argument to be without force. The greatest blemish of the present, the bondage of the peasants, cannot last much longer : " It is the peasants without property who, possessing only a hovel and their hands, depend for subsistence upon wages which are uncertain and always too small. It is these unfortunate people with whom the kind-hearted should be principally occupied. Condemned by their needs to submit to the will of the rich who employ them, they see their misery increased still more by the taxes, by the corvées, and above all, by the multiplicity of feast-days. . . . Such is the fate of the peasants in France. . . . But have we to regard it as a necessary evil, as an immediate consequence of the progress of society ? Certainly not ; it is a survival of barbarism which revolts us and which will not last long." [2]

In industry even today a much more cheerful picture presents itself. " All the workmen who are engaged in the mechanical arts have not only an assured subsistence, but also a fairly agreeable life. Even that class which seems to you the most deplorable, because they replace, so to speak, the beasts of burden (in London the coal-heavers and in Paris the market-porters) would not exchange their lot for easier work, because the high wages which they receive indemnify them for the fatigues which nature and habit have put them in a position to endure. . . . In a trading, industrial and well-ordered nation all men find employment. . . . The competition in the objects of labour increases the amount of wages and establishes a just balance between the rich man who consumes and the hireling who knows how to get himself paid." [3]

Chastellux is well aware, however, that this argument is not convincing. Even if it be true that the peasant will soon starve no longer and the worker is already no longer starving, even if it be true that the minimum necessary for existence is safeguarded for everyone, it by no means follows that the great differences of fortune in society have ceased to be a source of disturbance for social peace. What is, in Chastellux's own words, the argument of the enemies of the existing order ? " It is not given to men to judge otherwise than by comparison, and it is only

[1] II, 248.   [2] II, 250.   [3] II, 249–51.

on seeing men more fortunate than ourselves that we feel unhappy." [1]

"Well," answers Chastellux,[2] "I agree; but this is how I reason. If the pleasures [of the rich men] are always at hand, always habitual, they will not be pleasures long; and if he is a man who, without active and even somewhat uncertain sensations, desires the enjoyments of glory or those of love or the splendour of honours or public esteem, he must be an odd creature, strayed from the way of nature, whom it is well not to envy because he will be without activity and consequently unhappy. . . . One need not be far advanced in the moral sciences to know that happiness, on the whole, is compensated in the different classes of society; that courtiers and ministers are no happier than cultivators and artisans."

But, it may be further objected, "these different classes have at least seeming advantages". So much the better, Chastellux answers: "The desire and hope of passing from one to the other serve to maintain activity among men whom an assured subsistence would soon plunge into boredom and disgust. . . . As society is an immense camp where not only riches and enjoyments, but also desires and hopes should freely circulate, ny line of demarcation, any insurmountable barrier becomes an obstacle to the happiness of the greatest number." Here the state has to interfere: "The governments, after having made every effort to diminish the disproportion existing between the different classes of citizens, should endeavour to kindle emulation and hope by facilitating the transition from one [class] to the other. . . . Nothing is more favourable to the felicity of nations than the legislation of England, which makes everything accessible to merit and even to wealth." [3]

By granting this possibility of ascent the state safeguards internal peace; everything likewise must be done to preserve external peace. "The first blessing which a people should claim, is peace. Peace is the source of all order and of all good. What efforts for their happiness can those make who are occupied only with the care of attack and defence? . . . The first step to take towards the good of humanity would therefore be to make the periods of peace longer and wars fewer. . . . If it is true that the perfectibility of man and the progress of enlightenment will lead us one day to the greatest possible felicity . . . which will be the government that will best fulfil this task? This

[1] *Cf. supra.*   [2] II, 261 seq.   [3] II, 262 seq.

answer is easy : that which best maintains internal and external peace."¹

Is not the misery, past and present, which is usually laid to the charge of inequality, due in reality to the fact that there has hardly ever been true peace ? "From Clovis to Louis XIV, I see only the interval between the treaty of Vervins and the death of Henri IV [i.e. 1598–1610] which may be regarded as a period of real peace."²

But how are internal and external peace to be secured ? In his answer Chastellux once more approximates to the dominant opinion of his time. It is from an equilibrium of forces that he expects the prevention of war within and between states. "Man is born for liberty. . . . That liberty is in its essence indefinite and . . . can be limited in any individual only by that of another individual. . . . Whosoever envisages society from the true point of view will see only actions and reactions ; and whosoever attempts to form a correct idea of government will consider it as the equilibrium that ought to result from these actions and reactions ; so that, if we could make a solid and real system clearer by comparing it to an imaginary system . . . we should say that the moral world resembles the physical world of Descartes, where each vortex composed by a matter that tends always to move in a straight line is yet forced into a circular movement by the pressure of the neighbouring vortices."³

From this point of view the English form of government appears relatively the best : "In any mixed constitution the government is . . . only the result of the equilibrium of forces. In all other cases it is the dominance of a preponderant force, and that constitutes a state of war rather than a government."⁴

The form, however, does not matter, but only the thing : "Such is the importance and the necessity of counterpoises in the state that we should prefer to live in a monarchy where they would be well managed and always in action rather than under a democratic government where the will of the greatest number would have quick and immediate effect." For although we can envisage a social equilibrium in theory as well as an equilibrium of individual forces or an equilibrium of class forces, in practice only the latter alternative can be recommended : the equilibrium of individual forces is unstable, and only the equilibrium of class forces can last. "In fact, if you suppose a democracy where ranks and fortunes are rigorously equal, there is no need for a

---

¹ I, 27 seq. ; II, 271.   ² II, 56.   ³ I, 34 seq.   ⁴ II, 279 seq.

government, since no citizen has anything to envy or anything to take from his neighbour. But as this state of things is impossible or cannot last, property will soon be attacked and the rich will be at the mercy of the multitude until they have attached to themselves clients and can divide power ; and then there is already a contrast, an equilibrium ; such a state would be at least a sort of oligarchy or optimacy opposed to the multitude ; and if some understanding, some compromise, were arrived at, there would thenceforward be a mixture of aristocracy and democracy, an equilibrium of powers, a mutual supervision, in a word a mixed government." [1] Chastellux, an enlightened and philanthropic aristocrat, regarded an enlightened and philanthropic aristocracy as the best form of government.

In this conviction Chastellux seems not far from the opinion of his arch-adversary Mably. But in reality the contrast is sufficient : while Mably believed that the development of differences of fortune has led mankind from happiness to misery, Chastellux was convinced that the opposite was true of the history of civilized nations. Nowhere is this so manifest as in their judgments of the United States. While Mably prophesied an unhappy future for the young commonwealth because it did not, with Spartan rigour, force all men to adopt a like simplicity, Chastellux for the same reason was inclined to predict a favourable development for the thirteen colonies. This can be seen in the *Essay on Public Happiness*. " If we pass to North America ", he says, clearly aiming at Mably, the admirer of Antiquity, " we can defy the Solons and Lycurgus in opposing to them the Lockes and William Penns. Read the laws of Pennsylvania and Carolina and compare them to those of Sparta, and you will find the same difference as between the rule of St. Benedict and the domestic administration of a farm. Who would not experience an agreeable sensation in realizing that a territory of more than a hundred thousand square miles is now being populated under the auspices of liberty and reason, making equality the principle of its morals and agriculture that of its politics ? " [2]

These words were written, however, before Chastellux set foot on American soil. But the War of Independence brought him with Rochambeau's troops to the New World. Here he showed to his contemporaries the qualities of an excellent soldier. But he also found an opportunity of leaving to posterity a splendid proof of his remarkable gift of observation and philosophic

[1] II, 282 seq.   [2] II, 118 seq.

power of judgment : his book *Voyages dans l'Amérique septentrionale dans les années 1780, 1781 et 1782*,[1] composed of extracts from his diary. In spite of the details of military technique with which the account is encumbered it presents us with an interesting picture of the United States of 1776.

Conditions in the Northern States seemed to Chastellux to confirm the European conviction that America offered to the competent easy possibilities of ascent. " Any man who is able to procure a capital of five or six hundred livres of our money, or about twenty-five pounds sterling, and who has strength and inclination to work ", he relates of Connecticut,[2] " may go into the woods and purchase a portion of one hundred and fifty or two hundred acres of land, which seldom costs him more than a dollar or four shillings and six-pence an acre, a small part of which he pays in ready money. There he conducts a cow, some pigs, or a full sow, and two indifferent horses which do not cost him more than four guineas each. To these precautions he adds that of having a provision of flour and cyder. Provided with this first capital, he begins by felling all the smaller trees, and some strong branches of the large ones. . . . He next boldly attacks those immense oaks, or pines, which one would take for the ancient lords of the territory he is usurping ; he strips them of their bark. . . . It is enough for the small trees to be felled and the great ones to lose their sap. This object compleated, the ground is cleared ; the air and the sun begin to operate upon that earth which is wholly formed of rotten vegetables, and teems with the latent principles of production. . . . At the end of two years, the planter has wherewithal to subsist, and even to send some articles to market : at the end of four or five years, he completes the payment of his land, and finds himself a comfortable planter."

This rise to independent prosperity presupposed indeed not only hard labour, but also the disposal of a certain capital. Was not therefore the situation in the end the same as in Europe? By no means. Chastellux shows that it is easier in the New World than in the Old to advance from the state of a wage-earner to that of a petty capitalist. " Mr. Bullion ", he reports of an inn-keeper at Baskenridge in New Jersey,[3] " had two white servants, one a man about fifty, the other a woman, younger,

---

[1] The first part of this work, entitled *Voyage de Newport à Philadelphie*, was printed in 1782 aboard a French warship lying before Newport. This edition comprised only some twenty copies.
[2] *Travels in North America*, London 1787, I, 44 seq.   [3] I, 340 seq.

with a tolerable good face : I had the curiosity to enquire what wages he gave them, and was told that the man earned half a crown a day and the woman six shillings a week, or ten pence a day. If we pay attention to the circumstance, that these servants are lodged and fed, and have no expences, we may see that it is easy for them very shortly to acquire a piece of ground, and to form such a settlement as I have described."

In the industrial production of the Northern States, too, Chastellux saw growing welfare without social problems. " I took advantage of the good weather ", he relates of his stay at Farmington in Connecticut,[1] " to take a walk in the streets, or rather in the highways. I saw through the windows of a house that they were working at some trade ; I entered, and found them making a sort of camblet, as well as another woollen stuff with blue and white stripes for women's dress : these stuffs are sold at three shillings and six-pence the yard lawful money, or about two and twenty-pence English. The sons and grandsons of the family were at work : one workman can easily make five yards a day. The prime cost of the materials being one shilling currency, the day's work may amount to ten or twelve."

The whole tone of this vivid description shows that Chastellux regarded the social conditions in the country of the Yankees with approval. No wonder, as he saw the secret of social peace founded in the existence of easy possibilities of ascent. But in Dixie's land he beheld a different picture : " The Virginians differ essentially from the inhabitants to the north and eastward of the Bay (of Chesapeak) not only in the nature of their climate, that of their soil, and the objects of cultivation peculiar to it, but in that indelible character which is imprinted on every nation at the moment of its origin, and which by perpetuating itself from generation to generation, justifies the following great principles, that every thing which is, partakes of that which has been. . . . The first company which obtained the exclusive property of Virginia, was principally composed of men the most distinguished by their rank or birth. . . . It was natural therefore for these new colonists, who were filled with military principles, and the prejudices of nobility, to carry them into the midst even of the savages whose lands they were usurping . . . and the first impulse once given, it is not in the power of any legislator, nor even of time itself, wholly to destroy its effect. The government may become democratic, as it is at the present

[1] I, 38 seq.

moment; but the national character, the spirit of the government itself, will be always aristocratic." [1]

But not only in spirit, in reality also, Virginia, according to Chastellux's description, is a class state. " It is in this country that I saw poor persons, for the first time, after I passed the sea; for, in the midst of those rich plantations . . . miserable huts are often to be met with, inhabited by whites, whose wane looks, and ragged garments, bespeak poverty. At first I was puzzled to explain to myself, how, in a country where there is still so much land to clear, men who do not refuse to work, should remain in misery; but I have since learned, that all these useless territories, these immense estates, with which Virginia is covered, have their proprietors. Nothing is more common than to see some of them possessing five or six thousand acres of land, who clear out only as much as their negroes can cultivate; yet will they not give, nor even sell the smallest portion of them. . . ." [2] Hence in Virginia, in contrast to New England, there is a monopoly of the soil, and therefore, in spite of all political equality, social inequality must arise in this state.

The extensive cultivation of the soil in the Southern States, however, creates not only a class distinction between the whites, but also a class contrast between whites and blacks. Where great estates are to be worked, cheap labourers must be at hand. This, too, makes Virginia a class state. " Beneath this class of inhabitants, we must place the negroes, whose situation would be still more lamentable, did not their natural insensibility extenuate, in some degree, the sufferings annexed to slavery. . . . It is not only the slave who is beneath his master, it is the negro who is beneath the white man. No act of enfranchisement can efface this unfortunate distinction." [3] Only a mixture of races could make it disappear " until the colour should be totally effaced ".

Hence in the south of the Union, society was obviously split into classes. But even in the north a social stratification was about to develop, since not all citizens were in a position to profit to an equal degree from the liberty of ascent. Chastellux therefore felt that the great fact which characterized the society of the Old World must and would become a determining factor also in the New.

The problem of America as he saw it, Chastellux set forth in a letter to Professor Maddison of Williamsburgh which he

[1] II, 174–7.   [2] II, 190 seq.   [3] II, 193 seq., 199.

reprinted in his book : " The following, Sir," we read there,[1] " is a delicate question which I can only propose to a philosopher like you. In establishing amongst themselves a purely democratic government, had the Americans a real affection for a democracy ? And if they have wished all men to be equal, is it not solely because, from the very nature of things, they were themselves nearly in that situation ? For to preserve a popular government in all its integrity, it is not sufficient not to admit either rank or nobility, riches alone never fail to produce marked differences, by so much the greater, as there exist no others." The same idea he developed in a discussion with the great frondeur of Massachusetts of which he gave an ample account in his diary. " I expressed to Mr. Adams some anxiety for the foundations on which the new constitutions are formed, and particularly that of Massachusetts. Every citizen, said I, every man who pays taxes, has a right to vote in the election of representatives, who form the legislative body, and who may be called the sovereign power. All this is very well for the present moment, because every citizen is pretty equally at his ease, or may be so in a short time, but the success of commerce, and even of agriculture, will introduce riches amongst you, and riches will produce inequality of fortunes, and of property. Now, wherever this inequality exists, the real force will invariably be on the side of property ; so that if the influence in government be not proportioned to that property, there will always be a contrariety, a combat between the form of government, and its natural tendency, the right will be on one side, and the power on the other ; the balance then only can exist between the two equally dangerous extremes, of aristocracy and anarchy." [2]

Chastellux faithfully recorded the answer with which Samuel Adams tried to meet his objections. This is interesting because it shows how the fathers of the American constitution took the problem of the capitalistic class contrast into account, although it still belonged to a distant future. Adams does not seem to have believed in a natural harmony of interests in an industrial society ; but he was apparently convinced that they did not necessarily stand in opposition to each other. His fundamental idea was that of the older Bentham : the principle of the artificial identification of interests. " A state is never free but when each citizen is bound by no law whatever that he has not approved of, either by himself, or by his representatives. . . . It would be

[1] II, 346.   [2] I, 269 seq.

in vain for the people to possess the right of electing representatives, were they restrained in the choice of them to a particular class; it is necessary therefore not to require too much property as a qualification for the representative of the people." But this social democracy has its dangers. In order to restrain the effect of the people's pernicious passions which might one day show themselves, " it is necessary to moderate their first emotions, and bring them to the test of enquiry and reflection. This is the important business entrusted with the Governor and Senate" who thus fulfil the same functions as King and Upper House in England. These two constitutional powers, which cannot indeed prevent social upheavals, but are strong enough to retard them and thus to change political revolutions into legal evolutions, will in the future have to safeguard the interests of the economically richer minority against the poorer majority. " It is here we have given all its weight to property. A man must have a pretty considerable property to vote for a member of the Senate; he must have a more considerable one to be himself eligible. Thus the democracy is pure and entire in the assembly, which represents the sovereign; and the aristocracy, or, if you will, the optimacy, is to be found only in the moderating power, where it is the more necessary, as men never watch more carefully over the state than when they have a great interest in its destiny."[1] Thus equipped, Adams believed it possible confidently to face a future split of American society into antagonistic classes : " Such is the organization of our republic as to prevent the springs from breaking by too rapid a movement, without ever stopping them entirely."

This answer Chastellux seems to have regarded as a confirmation, rather than a refutation, of his objections, and he was right. For Adams was far from denying that the rise of a class contrast was unavoidable. On the contrary, he admitted that the constitution of his state reckoned with this necessity, and emphasized only that care had been taken to bring the growing antagonism to an issue in legal forms and gradual development. Thus Adams confirmed Chastellux in his conviction that the social harmony in the United States—however great it might appear at the time—would be of short duration.

" Some political writers, especially the more modern, have advanced, that property alone should constitute the citizen. They are of opinion that he alone whose fortune is necessarily

[1] I, 272 seq.

connected with its welfare has a right to become a member of the State. In America, a specious answer is given to this reasoning ; amongst us, say they, landed property is so easily acquired, that every workman who can use his hands, may be looked upon as likely soon to become a man of property. But can America remain long in her present situation ? And can the regimen of her infant state agree with her, now she has assumed the virile robe ? "[1] To put this question is to answer it in the negative : not always will a vast continent be at the disposal of a small people. The future will be painfully different from the present : " Such is the present happiness of America that she has no poor, that every man in it enjoys a certain ease and independence, and that if some have been able to obtain a smaller portion of them than others, they are so surrounded by resources, that the future is more looked to, than their present situation. . . . Now . . . let us suppose that the increase of population may one day reduce your artizans to the situation in which they are found in France and England. Do you in that case really believe that your principles are so truly democratical, as that the landholders and the opulent will still continue to regard them as their equals ? "[2] As soon as differences of possessions have arisen, political democracy becomes a meaningless form and indeed a dangerous fiction : " The ideal worth of men must ever be comparative : an individual without property is a discontented citizen. . . . What will result then, one day, from vesting the right of election in this class of citizens ? The source of civil broils, or corruption, perhaps both at the same time."[3]

Not only the fate of the state and society, but even that of culture in America depended upon the decision of the question, " whether the spirit of that democracy tends to the equality of fortunes, or is confined to the equality of ranks."[4] Chastellux's attitude to this point stands in undisguised opposition to his judgment of the social aspect of the same question. For while he regarded the class distinction of American society as socially harmful because it must destroy harmony in the state, he regarded it as culturally advantageous, because refinement from its very nature can only be the privilege of a small élite. His relation to social policy is characteristic of the contemporary of Rousseau ; his conception of cultural policy is typical of the grand seigneur who had grown up in the France of Louis XV. " It is melancholy to confess, that it is to a very great inequality in the dis-

[1] II, 345 seq.   [2] II, 347 seq.   [3] I, 270.   [4] II, 351.

tribution of wealth, that the fine arts are indebted for their most brilliant æras. In the time of Pericles, immense treasures were concentred in Athens, unappropriated to any particular purpose ; under the reign of Augustus, Rome owed her acquisition of the fine arts to the spoils of the world, if the fine arts were ever really naturalized at Rome."

From this point of view, the point of view of cultural philosophy and cultural critique, light and shadow seem to Chastellux distributed differently between North and South than from the point of view of social philosophy and social critique. Under this aspect Dixie's land appeared preferable to the home of the Yankees. " In the centre of the woods, and wholly occupied in rustic business, a Virginian never resembles an European peasant : he is always a freeman, participates in the government, and has the command of a few negroes. So that uniting in himself the two distinct qualities of citizen and master, he perfectly resembles the bulk of individuals who formed what were called the people in the ancient republics ; a people very different from that of our days, though they are very improperly confounded, in the frivolous declamations of our half philosophers, who, in comparing ancient with modern times, have invariably mistaken the word people, for mankind in general. . . . The dignity of man has been urged a hundred times, and the expression is universally adopted. Yet, after all, the dignity of man is relative ; if taken in an individual sense, it is in proportion to the inferior classes ; the plebeian constitutes the dignity of the noble, the slave that of the plebeian, and the negro that of his white master." [1] In this sense the true dignity of man is at home south of Mason and Dixon's line, where the country squire is opposed to his slave as in France the seigneur is to his subject.

Chastellux's aristocratic disinclination for the culture of the Northern States, primitively modest and egalitarian as it was, is most strikingly expressed in his judgment of the Quakers. In Philadelphia he met with one of their most famous representatives : " This Mr. Benezet may rather be regarded as the model, than as a specimen of the sect of Quakers : wholly occupied with the welfare of mankind, his charity and generosity made him be held in great consideration. . . . Of whatever sect a man may be who is inflamed with an ardent love of humanity, he is undoubtedly a respectable being ; but I must confess that it is difficult to bestow upon this sect in general, that esteem

[1] II, 56 seq.

which cannot be refused to some individuals. The law observed by many of them, of saying neither you, nor Sir, is far from giving them a tone of simplicity and candour. I know not whether it be to compensate for that sort of rusticity, that they in general assume a smooth and wheedling tone, which is altogether Jesuitical. Nor does their conduct belie this resemblance : concealing their indifference for the public welfare under the cloak of religion, they are sparing of blood, 'tis true, especially of their own people ; but they trick both parties out of their money, and that without either shame or decency. It is a received maxim in trade, to beware of them, and this opinion, which is well founded, will become still more necessary. In fact, nothing can be worse than enthusiasm in its downfall ; for what can be its substitute, but hypocrisy ? "[1]

Indeed, the bourgeois character of the New England Americans seemed to Chastellux to lead even to a degeneration of their most elementary means of expression, everyday language. " I got on horseback at eight o'clock on the 18th ", he relates,[2] " and at the distance of a mile fell in with the river of Farmington, along which I rode for some time. There was nothing interesting in this part of my journey, except that having fired my pistol at a jay, to my great astonishment the bird fell. . . . I must remark by the bye, that the Americans call it only by the name of the blue bird, though it is a real jay ; but the Americans are far from being successful in enriching their native language. On every thing which wanted an English name, they have bestowed only a simple descriptive one : the jay is the blue bird, the cardinal, the red bird ; every water bird is a duck, from the teal to the *canard de dois* and to the large black duck which we have not in Europe. They call them red ducks, black ducks, wood ducks. It is the same with respect to their trees ; the pine, the cypresses, the firs, are all comprehended under the general name of pine-trees. . . . I could cite many other examples, but it is sufficient to observe, that this poverty of language proves how much men's attention has been employed in objects of utility, and how much at the same time it has been circumscribed by the only prevailing interest, the desire of augmenting wealth. . . ."

The simple pleasures of rustic America seemed to him poor beside the refined entertainments of Paris and Versailles. He compares ; while in France fashionable society in the evening

[1] I, 278 seq., 282 seq.   [2] I, 41 seq.

goes to the Opera, in New Jersey they listen only to the song of the mocking-bird. And he draws the practical conclusion : " Great musicians are oftener to be met with in the courts of despots, than in republics. Here the songster of the night is neither the graceful Melico, nor the pathetic Tenducci ; he is the Bouffon Caribaldi : he has no song, and consequently no sentiment peculiar to himself : he counterfeits in the evening what he has heard in the day. Has he heard the lark or the thrush, it is the lark or the thrush you hear. Have some workmen been employed in the woods, or has he been near their house, he will sing precisely as they do. If they are Scotchmen, he will repeat you the air of some gentle and plaintive tale ; if they are Germans, you will discover the clumsy gaiety of a Swabian, or Alsatian. Sometimes he cries like a child, at others he laughs like a young girl : nothing, in short, is more entertaining than this comic bird." [1]

But however amusing this may be, it is only a beginning of culture, not culture proper : [only] " when music, and the fine arts come to prosper at Philadelphia ; when society once becomes easy and gay there . . . [only] then may foreigners enjoy all the advantages peculiar to their manners and government, without envying any thing in Europe." [2]

But is it not unjust to regard the culture of aristocratic France and luxurious Paris as the standard by which that of democratic America and her simple rustic life must be judged ? Was there not a culture of an entirely different character about to develop ? Not in Chastellux's view. For him there is but one ideal : " Perhaps it will be imagined . . . that rural life is best suited to mankind, contributing the most to their happiness, and the maintenance of virtue, without which there can be no happiness. But it must be remembered, that this same virtue, those happy dispositions, those peaceable amusements, we enjoy in the country, are not unfrequently acquisitions made in towns. If Nature be nothing for him who has not learnt to observe her, retirement is sterile for the man without information. Now this information is to be acquired best in towns. Let us not confound the man retired into the country, with the man educated in the country. The former is the most perfect of his species, and the latter frequently does not merit to belong to it." [3]

But although urban civilization is preferable to rural, it is not in all cities that true culture can be found. True culture

[1] I, 149 seq. [2] 294. [3] II, 352 seq.

is at home only in those towns where the landed gentry gather for social intercourse : " The arts, let us not doubt it, can never flourish, but where there is a great number of men. They must have large cities, they must have capitals. America possesses already five, which seem ready for their reception ; Boston, New-York, Philadelphia, Baltimore, and Charlestown. But they are sea-ports, and commerce, it cannot be dissembled, has more magnificence than taste ; it pays, rather than encourages artists."[1] This cannot be changed : " We must never flatter ourselves with hopes of modifying, after our pleasure, commercial towns. Commerce is more friendly to individual, than to public liberty, it discriminates not between citizens and strangers. A trading town is a common receptacle, where every man transports his manners, his opinions, and his habits ; and the best are not always the most prevalent. English, French, Italian, all mix together, all lose a little of their distinctive character, and in turn communicate a portion of it ; so that neither defects nor vices appear in their genuine light ; as, in the paintings of great artists, the different tints of light are so blended, as to leave no particular colour in its primitive and natural state." [2]

Thus it is only the image of Paris and France that Chastellux bears in his heart ; it is only the model of the culture of the *Ancien Régime* that he presents to the Americans as the ideal. " Shall I content myself with expressing to you my wishes ? " he asks Professor Maddison.[3] " I should desire that each state of America, as far as it is practicable, had a capital to be the seat of government, but not a commercial city. I should desire that their capital were situated in the centre of the republic, so that every citizen, rich enough to look after the education of his children, and to taste the pleasures of society, might inhabit it for some months of the year, without making it his only residence, without renouncing his invaluable country seat." Every American farmer a small baron—that is Chastellux's idea. " I should desire, in short, that in this capital and its appendage, the true national spirit might be preserved, like the sacred fire ; that is to say, that spirit which perfectly assimilates with liberty and public happiness."

[1] II, 352.   [2] II, 354 seq.   [3] II, 353 seq.

CHAPTER V

BRISSOT THE ADMIRER

The charming book of impressions and experiences which François-Jean de Chastellux published in 1786 was at once a lightly-drawn sketch and a profound critique of American society. Both these qualities caused it to be rejected by the European admirers of the thirteen states : on the one hand, the Marquis was accused of having treated his great subject too superficially, on the other he was denied the right to criticize the new commonwealth, because, as an aristocrat, he would be more inclined to blame than to praise. In fact, to the class-conscious bourgeoisie of France Chastellux's harmless diary of travels appeared not only frivolous, but even hostile, although it was neither the one nor the other. It was not long in the market before Jean Pierre Brissot attacked it in a vigorous pamphlet : the *Examen Critique des Voyages dans l'Amérique Septentrionale de M. le Marquis de Chatellux ; ou Lettre à M. le Marquis de Chatellux, dans laquelle on refute principalement ses opinions sur les Quakers, sur les Nègres, sur le Peuple, et sur l'Homme* (London).[1]

The United States of North America, Brissot de Warville points out, are to every progressive European an object of admiration : their example inspires the forces which are bent upon a rejuvenation and reform of the unnatural, unreasonable social order of Europe. To blame America is therefore to serve reaction. " And you, Sir, wish to destroy that enchantment ! You tacitly deny the correctness of those pictures ! Cruel man ! If it had been a delusion, ought you to destroy it ? It was dear

[1] The reading of this pamphlet may convey the impression that the contrast between Brissot and Chastellux was of a purely personal nature, that between a Cato and an Epicurus. Passages like the following seem to suggest this : " Even if you wish to flatter our French women you dishonour them. Here is the portrait which you sketch of them (Vol II, p. 97) : ' Not a movement without a grace, no grace without expression ; the desire of pleasing improves and perpetuates the means ; and Nature, rather aided than counteracted by Art, is never absolutely abandoned to a domestic life, nor lavished by an unlimited fecundity ' (Engl. trans. [1787], II, 126). " That is to say, in less florid but clearer French, that you congratulate our French women for being no longer either good housewives or mothers and for killing their posterity in order to have an elegant figure and to please their bachelor suitors. What a morality ! Good God ! And your book should fall into the hands of American women ! . . . May Heaven preserve those republics from a like depravation ! " (120 seq.). But behind the personal hides a social contrast, the contrast between Versailles and the Faubourgs of Paris, between luxury and labour, between nobility and the third estate.

to us, it was useful because it consoled the virtuous man and caused remorse to the vicious." [1] However, it cannot be assumed, it cannot be admitted, that Chastellux has spoken the truth : " It is not an illusion, it is realities, facts, which you attack." [2]

Brissot tries hard to refute Chastellux's critical considerations before himself and before others. He asserts that a member of the ruling states simply cannot be capable of grasping the greatness of the revolution which has taken place across the Ocean. " Your moral and religious opinions, your academical, military, and aristocratical spirit, this threefold *esprit de corps* . . . has it not made you from the outset a suspect witness and a partial judge ? " [3] Certainly, so much Brissot grants to his adversary, his book proves that he has wit. But even an excess of wit, nay, precisely an excess of wit, leads to a wrong judgment of the United States. For " wit . . . dries up the soul " and " it is with the soul that one should judge republicans, men of a pure morality . . ." [4]

The American commonwealth is an attempt to realize the ideal. Therefore one must be an idealist in order to understand it. But can a man like Chastellux who is at home in the fashionable salons be an idealist ? Of course not. " Those sweet reveries in which the soul is lost, that flight beyond the miserable husk which imprisons it, that sublime and consoling light which it thinks to perceive beyond itself, beyond our globe, in a better world . . . that state can only be the product of a perfect retirement into one's self, of a solitary and innocent life, and it is enjoyed only by those pure souls that are above the vain pleasures of this world and the petty objects of ambition." [5] The fight against Chastellux is therefore a war against immorality ; and a war against immorality has to be waged with severity : " The virtuous man should be severe. . . . The insolent should be pilloried." [6] These words not only contain the moral justification but indicate also the intellectual character of Brissot's pamphlet.

However, Brissot, in this little book, opposes Chastellux less with arguments than with declamations ; he speaks more as a shocked moralist than as a sober man of science. The reason is that, in 1786, Brissot did not yet know the United States. But it was not long before he came to know them : a few months later he himself crossed the Ocean for the land of promise, and

[1] *Examen*, 9.   [2] *Ib.*   [3] 12.   [4] 101, 21.   [5] 49.
[6] 129 seq.

in 1791 he published the work which here interests us most: the *New Travels in the United States of America performed in 1788*.[1]

To understand the concepts on which this book rests, it is now necessary to study Brissot's philosophic ideas. Like Raynal, like Mably, like Chastellux, Brissot was an important philosopher. What characterizes his thought is an uncompromising radicalism, a radicalism which is only content when it believes itself to have penetrated to the ultimate of things.

Now the ultimate of things, the original reality from which all others have sprung and to which all others can be traced, is the fact of motion. "All is in motion: life is its synonym."[2] Motion is in its essence creation. "That there is in the universe a certain quantity of motion, so much is proved by experience. The bodies which are but different modifications of matter, the principle in which this movement resides, are more or less strongly impregnated with it.... The bodies themselves are only products of motion. In fact, without it there is no mixture, no combination, and consequently no bodies."[3] But the opposite is equally true: creation is, in its essence, motion: "Is there an inner motion in matter, comprising all bodies, intrinsically working in them and constituting a part of their being?... To deny the existence of this motion in a stone, in the metals, because one does not see it, is like denying the circulation of blood, the internal fermentation which takes place in all fluids, because they are not seen.... This essential motion does not seem restricted to the realm of animals or plants alone; it embraces all matter and penetrates the smallest particle. It is the universal soul of the ancients."[4]

But if all life is motion, all life must be struggle; motion of independent bodies, it is clear, is impossible without collisions and conflicts. "All in this universe is thus endowed with the faculty of motion; and from the smallest particle of matter to the immense ball of the sun each body can apply its parts successively to the parts of another body, transport itself and be transported from one place to another. But such is the effect of this perpetual action and reaction of the bodies on each other: they change, they destroy each other; and since the principles of their being never fall into nothingness another body springs from

---

[1] *Nouveau voyage dans les États-Unis de l'Amérique Septentrionale, fait in 1788.* Trans. from the French, London, 1792.
[2] *Recherches Philosophiques sur le droit de propriété et sur le vol, considérés dans la nature et dans la société*, Bibliothèque Philosophique, VI (1782), 275, 268.
[3] 268.   [4] 268 seq.

their debris. . . . Thus the grass disappears under the teeth of the ox, reproduces itself in the form of his flesh, assumes another modality in the man who nourishes himself on beef and then disperses by evaporation or otherwise. . . . Motion involves action and reaction of bodies ; action involves destruction ; and in this perpetual combat of beings, the weaker succumbs to the stronger. . . ."[1]

So motion is not only creation but also annihilation. The two are indissolubly connected. Only together do they represent what we call life. " In this way the action and reaction of bodies produce those strange metamorphoses of form which we see at every moment. . . . It is in this succession, in this perpetual exchange of modes, that the universe finds its ornament. By destruction it is rejuvenated. . . . In its all-powerful hand the universe holds its life and death ; if its motion ceases, all is in apathy, nature is silent, the chaos spreads its sinister veil over it, and the end is near."

But if this is so, if annihilation is the beginning of the process, the consummation of which is called creation, then struggle must be recognized as a primeval fact, and the destruction of what is to be destroyed in the struggle must be regarded as necessary : " Hence all beings are under the necessity of moving and consequently of preserving their motion. This is a necessary result of their existence. . . . But since they cannot preserve their motion without affecting other bodies, and since this . . . brings about an infallible change of the parts of the one as well as the other, it follows that destruction is as necessary as preservation ; it follows that destruction leads to life, life to destruction. So two principles are certain and proved : (1) all beings must preserve their motions. (2) There is no preservation of motion in one body without destruction of others. From these two principles results a corollary just as certain, to wit that all bodies have the right to destroy each other. This is the right that is called property. . . . It is derived from the nature of things."[2]

In this way Brissot deduces the institution of property from a contemplation of the universe as a whole. Property is a central concept of life, not an invention of men. It far transcends the sphere of the merely social : all that strives to live needs property, and all that exists strives to live : in this respect all that exists and lives is equal. " If having wants is sufficient to make a proprietor, any individual that has wants may enjoy the right

[1] 270–2.   [2] 273 seq.

of property. . . . It is the same with the animals, they are proprietors exactly as man. . . . Have not the animals in fact, like us, their existence to preserve ? . . . Organization, needs, pleasures, sensations, all, all in them resemble our being ; and we should wish to deprive them of the right to all matter that nature has given them ! Unjust man, cease to be a tyrant ! The animal is thy equal, ay, thy equal. . . ." [1] Yet not only man and animal are alike, but even the animate and inanimate : " It is . . . certain that the plants have needs ; and if—as cannot be doubted—need is the only title to property which men and animals have, who could deprive them of the right to property ? If, like the animals, they have an appetence for those bodies which are most analogous to their nature and flee from those which harm them, do they not exercise this property ? . . . The result . . . is that all organized bodies are proprietors ; men, animals, plants." [2]

The right to property is thus conceived as the right to live : property is the most general right : all that exists has a right to property. But if this is so, then all that exists must be a possible object of property : " What can be subjected to the right of property ? Everything. Yes, man, animals, all bodies of nature have a right to everything. They have a right to each other. Man has a right to the ox, the ox to the grass, the grass to man. It is a combat of properties which would seem to tend to the destruction of nature, but which enlivens and rejuvenates it by destroying [mere] forms." [3] In other words, Brissot regards the struggle of all against all not only as the actual, but even as the legitimate principle of the coexistence of creatures. Indeed, he regards it as the principle of order and organization in the universe. " Ah ! if the animals would not destroy each other, what disorder would arise on the surface of this world ! There are in nature insects which pullulate without end like the greenflies which it is necessary to destroy if one does not wish to be destroyed by them. This reasoning can be applied to all animals both noxious and useful. If the herrings in the sea were allowed to multiply, if no carnivorous fish would feed on them, if no fisher would take them, these herrings, the number of which would infinitely increase, not finding enough nourishment, would perish and poison all. Nature has wisely provided against this inconvenience. The majority of fish take herrings for their food. . . . There is a just balance between propagation and depopula-

[1] 294 seq.   [2] 301 seq., 308.   [3] 309.

tion. Nature never fails herself." [1] Far-reaching consequences follow from this view, consequences from which Brissot does not shrink : " But . . . if the wolf may devour the sheep, if man has the faculty of nourishing himself from other animals, may it not be asked why the sheep, the wolf, and man should not equally have the right to make their fellows subservient to their appetites ? It will be objected that all beings have an invincible repugnance to lacerating, to devouring those of their species. In reply to an objection of this sort, the man of nature will lead him who raises it, into the woods ; he will show him the wolf drinking the blood of a wolf and satiating himself with his flesh ; he will show him a thousand animals, like rats, mice, hedgehogs who satisfy their appetite on their equals, their young. . . . He will conduct him to the cannibals ; and there, witness of those feasts of human flesh where even joy reigns, he will ask him what has become of this repugnance for the flesh of their fellows in all these beings. . . . The individuals of any species may therefore satisfy their appetites on the individuals of their own species by dint of the same reason for which they may do so with regard to the individuals other than their kind." [2]

These last considerations lead from the philosophy of nature to social philosophy. They seem to imply an unlimited individualism, and it cannot be doubted that the single individual with its elementary will to live represents the starting-point of Brissot's thought. " Property is the faculty possessed by the animal of using all matter for preserving its motion. This preservation is the centre of its needs. These needs thus are at the same time both end and title of property." [3] Nevertheless, Brissot's philosophy is by no means one-sidedly egoistic ; it is at the same time social : needs are not only the end and title of property—they are also its limit. " If Peter and Paul both claim the same thing, it is he who needs it for the preservation of his being who should carry it away and enjoy it. Where is the judge who has pronounced this principle, some lawyer will ask. Open the great book of nature and there you will find it. A river which runs in a bed wide enough to contain its waters, will it submerge the fields ? The oak which rises into the air, does it dispute with the reed a piece of soil that would be useless to it ? Yes, nature said and always will say to all beings whose needs are satisfied, Stop ! " [4] The earth has room

---

[1] 312 seq. [2] 313 seq., 317. [3] 274.
[4] 325.

for all.[1] Anyone may provide for his wants without harming his neighbour, for when he has taken what he needs, there is still wealth left in abundance.

But stay ! is this really true ? Are not the interests of men irreconcilable simply because their needs are unlimited ? The *natural* needs, Brissot answers, are by no means without limits, but, on the contrary, narrowly defined : if it seems to be different today, this is so only because the present social order is in opposition to the natural order of the universe. Thus Brissot's philosophy of nature turns into social critique : " If you wish to know what are the true wants of man, it is not our societies to which you must direct your eyes, it is primitive man ; social man shows almost no trace of nature. The needs of the savage are very few." This is proved by original societies with undepraved men : " In the beginning Greece was inhabited by the autochthons who entirely resembled the savages found in the forests of America. Fruit and the flesh of animals was their nourishment ; the skin of beasts, the bark of trees, their clothing ; the hollow of trees or a cave served them as shelter. . . . The inhabitants of Tierra del Fuego . . . live exactly in the state of nature. Their huts are formed from branches. Some grass spread in their hut serves them as beds ; . . . the extreme severity of the climate does not prevent them from going naked. Cockles and fish are their principal food." [2] This way of life is natural, any other unnatural : " Splendid Europeans, you hardly deign to notice these mortals who have too few wants to be able to reach your rank. But how much are they above you ! You degrade nature, but they preserve her in all her simplicity." [3] The commands of nature are plain and clear, " but social man does not obey nature. He widens, he extends his property beyond his wants ; he separates, he isolates himself, and he has the audacity to call this property sacred. . . . This is why. Man

---

[1] On this assumption depends all Brissot's optimistic social philosophy. When and where there is absolute scarcity, there develops a struggle of annihilation of the strong against the weak—even in the " state of nature." " There is just one case where the law of the stronger could be justly invoked and serve as the basis for the decision between two claimants : i.e., in the hypothesis that the need of Peter and Paul is equal. Both being equally forced to preserve the principle of their life, have an equal right to the thing which can prolong it : imagine two balls moved along the same line in contrary direction ; they meet, they strike against one another ; the heavier, the quicker, removes the other " (325 seq.). In this case we have before us an *affaire de statique* (*ib*). This, expressed without euphemism, probably means that in this case there is a blind struggle of brutal forces without pity. This is the weak spot of Brissot's social theory—and, in fact, of any social theory which tends to extol the order of nature above the moral laws of men.

[2] 285.   [3] 288.

has created for himself an immense quantity of factitious needs. His property has extended in proportion to his desires. He has broken the bounds which nature had set to his rights. Satisfied in his natural wants, he has preserved his property in order to satisfy his artificial demands. This was a true crime, because this preservation could not take place but at the expense of other individuals." [1] True wants alone give a natural right to property : " Examples . . . prove that the wants of man in the state of nature are very few in number. They have been extraordinarily multiplied in society. But in multiplying them the primitive right of property which nature has restricted to essential needs and some needs to which the climate gives rise has not been increased." [2] By the introduction of an artificial right of property which is not, like the natural right, confined to necessities, but goes far beyond them, society has been split into hostile classes : " Want is the limit of natural property. Civil property extends beyond superfluity. In nature everybody has a right to everything ; in society, a man to whom his parents leave no estate, has no right to anything. . . . Thus all the ideas of property which nature suggests have been confounded in society. The equilibrium which she established among all beings has been broken. Once equality was banished, those odious distinctions between rich and poor have been seen to arise. Society has been divided into two classes : the first that of possessing citizens living in idleness ; the second, more numerous, composed of the common people to which the right of existence has been sold dearly, which has been vilified, which has been condemned to perpetual labour." [3] How far it is from the present state of society to the original order of nature !

" If we wish to find a picture of the original way in which men exercised their right of property, it is presented to us by the animals. Zealous to satisfy the wants which nature gives them, they do not seek to call forth others. They are content with what chance offers them for their nourishment and preservation. They do not commit the folly of spoiling the offerings of nature by artificial preparation. The animal way of life is simple, as all their desires are moderate, and they have enough never to covet anything. Their needs satisfied, they do not regard themselves as proprietors of a portion of matter which is useless to them." [4] The contrast is striking : " The essence . . . of natural property is its being universal. Social property is

[1] 322, 329.   [2] 286.   [3] 332.   [4] 296 seq.

individual, particular ; hence these two rights are absolutely antagonistic." ¹ And the opposition between natural and social is at the same time the opposition between good and bad : " Parting from nature is depravation." ² Unjustly does the rich man call what he holds his property : it is not his property in the high, the true, the natural sense of the word : " Haughty man who, swimming in the midst of opulence, disdainfully insultest the miserable wretch whom thou hast robbed, cease grandiloquently to describe thy usurpations by the name of property ! . . . Yes, these trenches, these walls with which thou surroundest thy immense parks ; these bars which prohibit access to thy estates ; all prove thy tyranny, and nothing thy property. . . . At thy door a hundred unhappy people die of hunger. . . . The provisions that are in thy houses, the wine that is in thy cellars : all is theirs. . . . This is the law of nature." ³

However, these words must not be interpreted as if Brissot wished to advocate a communist order of society. Communism, he holds, is possible, but only under primitive conditions : " At Sparta, who would believe it ? a civilized nation, all was in common. Lycurgus had studied nature, he imposed her laws on his fellow-citizens, and he realized in part the beautiful dream of the Platonic state. . . . I do not, however, undertake to apply the rigid legislation of Lycurgus to the immense kingdom of France. Conceived with wisdom for the small territory to which it was confined, it would be impossible to execute it in a vast empire. It has for its base the abolition of all property, equality among the citizens ; and this equality will never be more than a chimera with a people that is at once agricultural, trading, and numerous. . . . An equal partition of property would be impossible and illusory ; for a short interval of time would see the reappearance of that inequality the proscription of which had been intended. So it is not by this chimerical means that we must seek to make men happy." ⁴ In fact, nature must not be understood in this sense. " It would be an error to believe that in nature there should be a perfect equality in property. Not all animals have an equal number of needs. Some are stronger, others weaker ; the ones digest more quickly, the others have several stomachs and those very large. Nourishment being proportional to wants, it follows that the right of property is greater, more extensive, in certain animals. The system of equality of property is, therefore, from this point of

¹ 324.   ² *Examen*, 93.   ³ *Recherches*, 289 seq.   ⁴ 291, 32 seq.

view, a chimera which one would in vain try to realize among men. Although they are similar by their organization, this differs in many respects. Their needs are not the same. A Pythagorean lived on vegetables. . . . Milo ate a bull in a day. Hence as the needs of men differ, be it in quality or in quantity, they cannot be proprietors to the same extent. Therefore this system of equality of fortunes which certain philosophers have wished to establish, is false in nature." [1] Brissot was a bourgeois philosopher : " We lay down ", he says,[2] " as the foundation of good legislation the safety of property both personal and landed."

An equality among men on the basis of a wide distribution of the material wealth of mankind : that was the ideal after which Brissot strove. Is there any hope of realizing it ? In the depth of his heart Brissot answered this question in the negative as far as Europe was concerned, and he sometimes even admitted it : " It would be necessary to distribute the riches in a just proportion among the citizens. . . . But, once more, these romantic ideas must be relegated, with the fable of the golden age, to the poetical dreams. . . . There will always be rich : hence there must be poor as well. In well-governed states these latter work and live ; in the others, they don the rags of mendicancy and insensibly undermine the state under the cloak of idleness. Let us then have poor, but let us never have beggars ; that is the end towards which a good administration should strive." [3]

The measures for the solution of the social problem which Brissot suggests are therefore very restricted. " If it should happen that a district overflows with too extensive a population. . . . I should say : let us send this surplus population to the deserts of America to cultivate the Appalachians." [4] The essential thing is to offer the proletarian a possibility of gaining his bread and, if possible, of rising. The task of legislation is virtually fulfilled " if the unfortunate whom chance has brought into the world without property, though with wants, may, by his work, correct the injustice of fate and efface the inequality in the distribution of wealth ; if moreover the fruit of his labour does not become the prey of the greedy tax-collector. The rich may then be rich with impunity because desperation will no longer press its knife into the hands of the indigent whom his

---

[1] 291 seq. [2] 31. [3] 69.
[4] *Théorie des Lois Criminelles*, 1781, II, 59.

proud opulence has insulted." [1] This therefore is Brissot's ultimate counsel : " Give to those who have not got it, property or employment ; this is the true secret "—the true secret of a wise art of government.

However, the postulate " bread for all " only shows the way out of the deepest misery. The postulate " property for all " indicates the way to the highest ideal. " It must be admitted . . . that property is far preferable to employment in factories." [2] Here lies the great, the decisive difference between the old and the new world : " The Americans are and will be for a long time free ; it is because nine-tenths of them live by agriculture ; and when there shall be five hundred millions of men in America, all may be proprietors." [3] Practice proves this : " When the number of farmers is augmented in any canton beyond the number of convenient farms the population languishes, the price of land rises to such a degree as to diminish the profits of agriculture, encourage idleness, or turn the attention to less honourable pursuits. The best [and, in America, the natural] preventative of these evils is the emigration of part of the inhabitants. This part generally consists of the most idle and dissipated, who necessarily become industrious in their new settlement ; while the departure augments the means of subsistence and population to those left behind ; as pruning increases the size of the tree, and the quantity of its fruit." [4] In Europe such a recurring rejuvenation of society is out of the question : " We are not in that happy situation in France : the productive lands in France amount to fifty millions of acres ; this, equally divided, would be two acres to a person ; these two acres would not be sufficient for his subsistence." A considerable part of the French will therefore always be compelled to seek their bread by industry. " The nature of things calls a great number of the French to live in cities." This is most unfortunate : the European " societies are condemned to be infested with great cities . . . [and] misery and vice are the necessary offspring of these cities ". [5]

These considerations make it clear how Brissot wished to see the United States constituted : as a commonwealth of independent farmers in which industry should play little or no part. Certainly—in this respect he was under no illusion—even industries arise by a spontaneous process of development ; there-

---

[1] *De la France et des États-Unis*, ed. 1791, 30.   [2] *Ib.*, 86.
[3] *New Travels*, xxi.   [4] *Ib.*, 338.   [5] *Ib.*, xxii, 205 seq.

fore they cannot simply be rejected as harmful, since the natural and the good are identical. But there are different kinds of industry, and not all are natural and good : " If we attentively consider the nature of man we see that it leads him unceasingly towards the means of rendering his life agreeable. . . . Let us therefore agree that, by his nature, man tends towards enjoyments and consequently towards manufactures. Manufactures, like the desires of civilized men, may be divided into three classes : to wit, (1) those of necessity, (2) those of comfort, (3) those of luxury or fancy. . . . If man no longer wants anything for his comfort, he thinks of decoration. Then arise the desires of luxury ; they rest entirely on imagination. The nature of these three kinds of wants determined, we must see which are those entertained by the free Americans : they have the two former. . . . Their situation, their austere religion, their morals, their ancient customs, their rural or seafaring life turn the free Americans in general away from artificial pomp, ostentation, and voluptuousness." [1]

The future development, the future happiness of the United States, Brissot holds, depends upon the question whether it will be possible to keep the industrial sector of economic life small —whether it will be possible to preserve modesty in wants and simplicity of life. This is the decisive question. It is in the last resort a question of morals. What is the attitude of the Americans themselves ? The answer, he points out, is different in North and South. " If we speak of luxury with respect to free America, great care must be taken to distinguish the states of the South from those of the North. . . . There is certainly luxury in Virginia. . . . However, the evil is not yet perceptible, at least in the states of the North." [2]

Thus Brissot, too, ascribes great importance to the contrast between North and South. He is aware that it is a contrast which has its roots in the social sphere : the contrast between egalitarian New England and the slavery states with their aristocracy and class domination. As symbolic of the character of the Northern republics he took Connecticut. " This state ", he says,[3] " owes all its advantages to its situation. It is a fertile plain, inclosed between two mountains, which render difficult its communications by land with the other states. . . . Agriculture being the basis of the riches of this state, they are here

[1] *De la France et des États-Unis*, ed. 1791, 101 seq.   [2] *Ib.*, 102.
[3] *New Travels*, 133.

more equally divided. There is here more equality, less misery, more simplicity, more virtue, more of every thing which constitutes republicanism." South of the Mason-Dixon line a totally different picture presents itself : " With the State of Delaware finishes the system of protection to the blacks. . . . When you run over Maryland and Virginia you conceive yourself in a different world ; and you are convinced of it, when you converse with the inhabitants. They speak not here of projects for freeing the negroes. . . . The strongest objection lies in the character, the manners and habits of the Virginians. They seem to enjoy the sweat of slaves. They are fond of hunting ; they love the display of luxury, and disdain the idea of labour." [1] The consequences are obvious : " You will not find there those cultivated plains, those neat country-houses, barns well distributed, and numerous herds of cattle, fat and vigorous. No : every thing in Maryland and Virginia wears the print of slavery : a starved soil, bad cultivation, houses falling to ruin, cattle small and few, and black walking skeletons ; in a word you see real misery, and apparent luxury, insulting each other." [2]

Yet the difference between North and South, between Connecticut and Virginia is to Brissot less economic and social than moral and cultural. Here the deep contrast between him and Chastellux comes to light, the contrast between nobility and bourgeoisie, between Versailles and the Faubourgs of Paris. The one despises what is admired by the other. Nevertheless, they share their intellectual starting-point. Great though the rational and irrational antagonism between Chastellux and Brissot may be, in one respect, perhaps the most important, they agree ; in their philosophical judgment of the cultural fertility of classless and class society. Brissot, in fact, believed with Chastellux that only where fortunes are unequally distributed can there arise a splendid blossoming of science and art. But his order of values is different. In opposition to Chastellux he is convinced that the pleasures of cultural life cannot outweigh the pains of social inequality. At Boston he met a certain Mr. Pope, who had constructed an ingenious Planetarium, but saw himself forced to think of emigration, because he could not find his bread in America. " This discouraged artist told me one day ", he relates,[3] " that he was going to Europe to sell this machine, and to construct others. This country, said he, is too poor to encourage the arts. These words ' this country is too

[1] *Ib.*, 280 seq.　　　[2] *Ib.*, 288.　　　[3] *Ib.*, III seq.

poor', struck me. I reflected, that if they were pronounced in Europe, they might lead to wrong ideas of America; for the idea of poverty carries that of rags, of hunger; and no country is more distant from that sad condition. When riches are centred in a few hands, these have a great superfluity; and this superfluity may be applied to their pleasures, and to favour the agreeable and frivolous arts. When riches are equally divided in society, there is very little superfluity, and consequently little means of encouraging the agreeable arts. But which of these two countries is the rich, and which is the poor? According to European ideas, and in the sense of Mr. Pope, it is the first that is rich; but, to the eye of reason, it is not; for the other is the happiest. Hence it results, that the ability of giving encouragement to the agreeable arts, is a symptom of national calamity." The happiness of the Americans is not what the depraved Europeans regard as happiness: the culture of the Americans is not what the Europeans conceive as culture. " The happiness of a Pennsylvania farmer ... offers not the pleasures of the Arcadia of the poets, or those of the great towns of Europe; but it promises you independence, plenty, and happiness—in return for patience, industry, and labour. The moderate price of lands, the credit that may be obtained, and the perfect security that the courts of justice give to every species of property, place these advantages within the reach of every condition of men." [1] And the happiness of the Americans is true happiness: the culture of the Americans is true culture. " It is in a country life in America, that true happiness is to be found by him who is wise enough to make it consist in tranquillity of soul, in the enjoyment of himself, and of nature. What is the fatiguing agitation of our great cities, compared to this delicious calmness? The trees, my friend, do not calumniate, they revile not their benefactors; men of the greatest merit cannot always say this of their fellow-creatures." [2]

Alas! The Southern States are far removed from this true culture. Brissot himself had to experience this, and it distressed him. " The President of Congress, Mr. Griffin ... is a Virginian, of very good abilities, of an agreeable figure, affable, and polite. I saw at his house, at dinner, seven or eight women, all dressed in great hats, plumes, &c. It was with pain that I remarked much of pretension in some of these women; one acted the giddy, vivacious; another, the woman of sentiment. This last

[1] *Ib.*, 336. [2] *Ib.*, 445 seq.

had many pruderies and grimaces. Two among them had their bosoms very naked. I was scandalized at this indecency among republicans." [1] A thorough reform of morals is needed here : " You must banish idleness and the love of the chace, which are deeply rooted in the soul of the Virginians; and, above all things, you must banish slavery; which infallibly produces those great scourges of society, laziness and vice, in one class of men, unindustrious labour and degrading misery in another." [2] Culturally as well as socially the states of the South are reminiscent of the European model. Like Europe they must be reformed. They may be on the way to the ideal—they are certainly not near it.

The states of the North, indeed, are different : they are as near to the ideal as things human can possibly be. " The Bostonians ", says Brissot,[3] " unite simplicity of morals with that French politeness and delicacy of manners which render virtue more amiable. . . . Music, which their teachers formerly proscribed as a diabolic art, begins to make part of their education. In some houses you hear the forte-piano. This art, it is true, is still in its infancy; but the young novices who exercise it are so gentle, so complaisant, and so modest, that the proud perfection of art gives no pleasure equal to what they afford. God grant that the Bostonian women may never, like those of France, acquire the malady of perfection in this art ! It is never attained, but at the expence of the domestic virtues."

Brissot's democratic and egalitarian predilection for the Northern States, is most clearly manifest in his judgment of the Quakers. It is in the discussion of this sect, its merits and its faults, that he accuses the " frivolous academician " Chastellux of having written " for the sake of gaining the infamous applauses of the parasites of despotism "—and, indeed, " to please the pretty graceful women of Paris ".[4] He sees them in a totally different light : as ideal types of a new, of bourgeois man, compared with whom the product of the feudal society of France must appear miserable and despicable. " Simplicity, candour, and good faith, characterize the actions as well as the discourses of the Quakers. They are not affected, but they are sincere ; they are not polished, but they are humane ; they have not that wit, that sparkling wit, without which a man is nothing in France and with which he is everything ; but they have good sense, a sound judgment, an upright heart, and an obliging temper of

[1] *Ib.*, 169.   [2] *Ib.*, 445.   [3] *Ib.*, 94 seq.   [4] *Ib.*, 263, 390.

mind. If I wished to live in society, it would be with the Quakers : if I wished to amuse myself, it would be with my countrymen. And their women—you ask, what are they? They are what they should be.... Their principal characteristic is that they are not eager to please all the world : neglectful of the exterior, they reserve all their accomplishment for the mind. Let us say it, let us not cease to repeat it, it is among manners like these that we are to look for good households, happy families, and public virtues." [1] The Quakers have succeeded in closing the source of evil : " Three kinds of vice or rather of crime have brought about all the suffering that desolates the earth.... They are ambition, cupidity, luxury. Now, the Quakers have no ambition because they renounce all power ; they have no cupidity, [for] it would be senseless ; they have no luxury. Here then is . . . the sect of humanity." [2]

What Brissot admires in the Quakers is their simplicity. The modest man who, as far as possible, reduces his wants to the minimum is to him, as we have seen, the new, the natural, the ideal man. Simplicity, bourgeois simplicity, is the essential feature of the Quakers. Even their form of worship demonstrates this. " The history of the Quakers will prove the falsity of a principle often advanced in politics. It is this : that, to maintain order in society, it is necessary to have a mode of worship striking to the senses ; and that the more show and pomp are introduced into it, the better. . . . Two or three hundred thousand Quakers have none of these mummeries, and yet they observe good order. . . . In considering the simplicity of the Quakers' worship . . . I have been surprised that the Society should maintain a concurrence with more brilliant sects, and even increase by making proselytes from them. This effect is principally to be attributed to the singular image of domestic happiness which the Quakers enjoy. Renouncing all external pleasures, music, theatres, and shows, they are devoted to their duties as citizens, to their families, and to their business ; and thus they are beloved with their wives, cherished by their children, and esteemed by their neighbours. Such is the spectacle which has often drawn to this Society men who have ridiculed it in their youth." [3]

This simplicity of the Quakers is, however, not confined to their houses : it tends, as a counterpoise to luxury, to become a social principle. Thus it helps to preserve the good and to

[1] *Ib.*, 376 seq. [2] *Examen*, 76 seq. [3] *New Travels*, 199 seq.

prevent the bad : " No Society does more for the public good [than that of the Friends]. It is owing to them, that Philadelphia has hitherto been preserved from the danger of theatres. Their petition this year, to prevent permission being obtained to erect one, has been successful." [1] It would be unjust, Brissot contends, to condemn this attitude as hypocritical : " Public felicity may be attained without singing and springing on the boards." [2] Indeed, " the death of a wolf is more important for the common well-being than the Opera of Paris ".[3]

Now for this sober and austere but solid and secure bourgeois culture of the Northern States Brissot sees one great danger : the danger of wealth. Wealth engenders luxury, and luxury corruption : true happiness lies half-way between want and opulence. Brissot was a bourgeois, but he was a petty bourgeois. He was an individualist, but he was an egalitarian. His ideal was a society of peasants and artisans, not a society of rich and poor. In agriculture and handicrafts great differences of wealth cannot arise because the prospects of success are the same for all. It is different in commerce, which holds unlimited possibilities for the speculator. Brissot was therefore, like Chastellux, if for different reasons, an adversary of trading cities. " In countries chiefly devoted to commerce, the sciences are not carried to any high degree. This remark applies to Boston. . . . Science is not diffused among the inhabitants of the town. Commerce occupies all their ideas, turns all their heads, and absorbs all their speculations." [4] Even the citadel of the new culture, the Philadelphia of the Quakers, is already contaminated by the poisonous spirit of commerce : " The inhabitants [of the City of Brothers] wish for the aggrandizement of their city : they are wrong ; Philadelphia is already too considerable. When towns acquire this degree of population, you must have hospitals, prisons, soldiers, police, spies, and all the sweeping train of luxury ; that luxury which Penn wished to avoid. It already appears : they have carpets, elegant carpets ; it is a favourite taste with the Americans ; they receive it from the interested avarice of their old masters, the English. The Quakers have likewise carpets ; but the rigorous ones blame this practice. A carpet in summer is an absurdity ; yet they spread them in this season, and from vanity : this vanity excuses itself by saying that the carpet is an ornament ; that is to say, they sacrifice

---

[1] *Ib.*, 409.   [2] *Examen*, 67.   [3] *De la France et des États-Unis*, 176.
[4] *New Travels*, 109 seq.

reason and utility to show." [1] In other places of the Northern States the seductive influence of the trading spirit is still more apparent. " If there is a town on the American continent where the English luxury displays its follies, it is New York. . . . The inhabitants are far from complaining at it; they prefer the splendour of wealth, and the show of enjoyment, to the simplicity of manners, and the pure pleasures resulting from it. The usage of smoking has not disappeared in this town. . . . The philosopher condemns it, as it is a superfluous want. . . . You will find here the English fashions. In the dress of the women, you will see the most brilliant silks, gauzes, hats, and borrowed hair. . . . The men have more simplicity in their dress; they disdain gewgaws, but they take their revenge in the luxury of the table. Luxury forms already, in this town, a class of men very dangerous in society—I mean bachelors. The expence of women causes matrimony to be dreaded by men." [2]

The defence of the new culture against this disintegrating element—this is the problem of the American community. " Everywhere in the United States the question is discussed : how to set limits to foreign trade ? how arrest the progress of luxury ? Stay at home, till the soil, till the soil, is our advice. This is the secret by which you delay the advance of luxury. . . . This arises in towns from satiety, idleness and ennui. Work preserves the country from these moral maladies." [3] Only if American society remains ethically strictly puritan, and socially pre-eminently agrarian, can the ideal be saved : " In the republics those costly productions should be carefully avoided which, shifting property into a small number of hands, bring about great variations of fortunes. Economy, simplicity, private virtues agree ill with such differentiated possessions. They can be found only in the sphere of mediocrity, of easy circumstances founded on labour whose produce is secure. This is generally the case with agriculture." [4]

Thus the social ideal of the revolutionary Brissot leads to a conservative (in fact, we might almost say to a reactionary) social policy. This fact exposes the whole problem of the programme of the liberal bourgeoisie. Brissot wished to overcome the feudal contrast of estates, but at the same time to nip in the bud the capitalist contrast of classes ; he wished to set the wheel of history going and then arrest it in full swing—an aim as sub-

[1] *Ib.*, 317.   [2] *Ib.*, 155–7.   [3] *De la France et des États-Unis*, 119, 121.
[4] *Ib.*, 134 seq.

lime as it was fantastic, as great as it was impossible : " Health and benevolence have diminished on this earth in proportion to the increase of manufactures, towns, great properties, and the abandonment of rural life, and ... vices and crimes have increased in the same measure. ... The idea of property is one of the strongest bonds that bind man to life, to his country, to virtue, one may even say, to health. It is far, very far, from the satisfaction of a factory employee, who, at the end of the week, finds himself proprietor of a louis, to that of a small rural proprietor who seldom holds this sum but, day by day, sees all he needs growing in his own field. ... The labourer is good because he depends only on the soil which yields to him liberally and willingly, while the interest of the master who pays the factory worker always mingles the bitterness of enmity with the payment which he receives. The labourer is good because he lives only among equals ; for inequality is the source of all wickedness ; the superior is wicked because he wishes to uphold his oppression ; the slave is wicked because he wishes to destroy it and to avenge himself. The labourer is good and even generous because it would be necessary to abandon all cultivation, if there were no reciprocity of services and confidence among the cultivators."[1]

Brissot does not hesitate to draw the practical conclusions from this opinion : he recommends that commerce and industry should be kept small, as their development would threaten the social democracy and the democratic felicity in the states : " In preventing, or at least retarding, the birth of manufactures within their frontiers, the United States would retard the decadence of morals and of public spirit ; for if the manufactures attract gold to the States, they attract at the same time a poison which undermines them. They gather a multitude of individuals whose physique and morals decline together ; they accustom and form man for servitude ; they give in the republics preponderance to aristocratic habits, tastes, ideas, and desires ; in a word, by accumulating wealth in a small number of hands, they incline the republics towards aristocracy."[2] Indeed, he goes even further : he warns the Americans not to come into contact with Europe, lest a bad example should spoil good morals. " From the same point of view the free Americans would also act wisely ... if they little frequented the ports and cities of the ancient continent. In fact, the European arriving in Free America is about but one in a hundred, and sometimes a thousand. His

[1] *Ib.*, 110–12. [2] *Ib.*, 116.

example has therefore only very small influence; the luxury which he displays in passing excites less consideration or respect than disdain or ridicule. . . . The opposite takes place if a free American lands in Europe. Almost alone . . . he finds himself thrown into an atmosphere of habits contrary to his own. So he must little by little become familiar with them. . . . Importing this mental disposition into his home-land, he makes it insensibly pass into the souls of those who surround him. . . . Thus he weakens by his example their taste for simplicity and the coming century sees the public virtues vanish into indifference." [1]

If these precautions are taken—if contamination from the social disease called luxury is prevented and its germ within the Union destroyed—bourgeois society and bourgeois culture can and will flourish in America. Brissot is confident; he believes that there is ground for confidence. The very economic conditions are so constituted as to keep the country agricultural and therefore egalitarian : " Those whom ambition, or cupidity, or ignorance should make inclined to establish manufactures will be infallibly turned away from this plan by the dearness of manual labour. This dearness . . . is very great. . . . For a long time to come there will be more to gain in the United States from the soil which yields with abundance than in factories, and man turns where he hopes for greater and quicker profits. As the population will, for some centuries, be out of proportion to the size of the United States, the soil there will still be cheap for a long time and consequently its inhabitants will for long be cultivators." [2]

Even Virginia, the country of luxury, the country of inequality, Brissot believes to be on the way to improvement : the Virginians " think slaves necessary only for the cultivation of tobacco : [but] this culture declines and must decline in Virginia. The tobacco of the Ohio and the Mississippi is more abundant, of a better quality, and requires less labour. When this tobacco shall open its way to Europe, the Virginians will be obliged to cease from this culture and ask of the earth, wheat, corn, and potatoes ; they will make meadows, and rear cattle. . . ." The substitution of the sugar-maple for the sugar-cane will also tend to make slavery unnecessary. " It is perhaps more owing to this consideration than to humanity, that you see free labour introduced in a part of Virginia, in that part bordered by the beautiful river Shenadore. In travelling here, you will think yourself in

[1] *Ib.*, 117 seq.   [2] *Ib.*, 113.

Pennsylvania. Such will be the face of all Virginia, when slavery shall be at an end." [1]

Thus Brissot, in spite of all the dangers that he sees, looks hopefully into the future. Indeed, his expectations carry him away. O kindly seer, how blinded was thine eye! " I transport myself sometimes in imagination to the succeeding century. I see this whole extent of continent, from Canada to Quito, covered with cultivated fields, little villages, and country houses. (America will never have enormous cities like London and Paris ; which would absorb the means of industry and vitiate morals. Hence it will result, that property will be more equally divided, population greater, manners less corrupted, and industry and happiness more universal.) I see Happiness and Industry, smiling side by side, Beauty adorning the daughter of Nature, Liberty and Morals rendering almost useless the coercion of Government and Laws, and gentle Tolerance taking [the] place of the ferocious Inquisition. I see Mexicans, Peruvians, men of the United States, Frenchmen, and Canadians, embracing each other, cursing tyrants, and blessing the reign of Liberty, which leads to Universal Harmony." [2]

[5] *New Travels*, 288 seq. [6] *Ib.*, 482 seq.

CHAPTER VI

THE PROBLEM OF AMERICA

However different the temperaments of the four authors whom we have considered, however different the opinions by which they were governed, they all agreed on one point : the conviction that the United States of America would not always remain the ideal country of liberty and equality. What Raynal with equanimity regarded as inevitable, what Mably in discouragement predicted as necessary, what Chastellux critically and coolly weighed in its advantages and disadvantages, and Brissot feared without openly admitting it, occurred : the development of class contrasts on the basis of differences of fortune, the outbreak of a class struggle between rich and poor, capitalist and proletarian. Yet the change took place more quickly even than the worst pessimists had expected. The plutocracy of the new rich did not evolve through long decades, but was artificially created in a few years. The historical opposition between Hamilton and Jefferson, the bitter contest between Federalists and Republicans, was the political reflection of this process.

Rarely has a legislative assembly done more to promote the creation of a capitalist upper class than the first Congress of the United States. The resolution to redeem the public debt to its full nominal amount after the bonds had fallen to a tenth of their value and had been bought up at this mock price by a little group of bold speculators acted as much against the small man as the rigorous introduction and exaction of commodity taxes and import duties. When, in the year 1800, the political current turned, the great change had already taken place.

Although only a question of party politics seemed to be under discussion, the conviction was general that the social future of the whole continent was at stake. Egalitarian state or class state—that was the problem of America. Both ideas found valiant champions : the egalitarian state in John Taylor of Caroline, the class state in John Adams, Washington's successor. Their writings are the echo of the European discussions of the United States, an echo, however, which far surpasses the original in strength and realism.

John Adams embodied his doctrine in *A Defence of the Constitutions of Government of the United States of America* (1787). This book may be described as the intellectual pioneer of the capitalist class state in the New World.

Equality, equality of property, John Adams points out, cannot exist. It would presuppose equal abilities, equal devotion, equal diligence. In reality, however, the majority of men are indolent and only a minority industrious. " There is in every nation and people under heaven a large proportion of persons who take no rational and prudent precautions to preserve what they have, much less to acquire more. . . . Suppose a nation . . . ten millions in number, all assembled together ; not more than one or two millions will have lands, houses or any personal property." For " indolence is the natural character of man ", at least of average man, the man of the multitude.[1] A state of social equality could therefore never arise spontaneously. But even if artificially introduced, it would not last. Suppose in a country " a downright equal division of every thing be demanded, and voted. What would be the consequence of this ? The idle, the vicious, the intemperate, would rush into the utmost extravagance of debauchery, sell and spend all their share, and then demand a new division of those who purchased from them." [2] Men's ardour for equality must not be misunderstood : it is purely negative and never positive ; it is directed, not towards the raising of the lower, but to the lowering of the higher states. " Every man hates to have a superior, but no man is willing to have an equal. . . . No man will ever acknowledge himself to be upon a level or equality with others, till they are brought down lower than him." [3]

In the end it is with equality of goods exactly as with community of wives : " Such reveries may well be called delirious, since, besides all the other arguments against them, they would not extinguish the family spirit or produce the equality proposed ; because, in such a state of things, one man would have twenty wives, and one woman twenty lovers, while others would languish in obscurity, solitude, and celibacy." [4]

Thus the existence of class differences must be conceived and accepted as a necessity of nature. " The people, in all nations, are naturally divided into two sorts, the gentlemen and the simplemen, a word which is here chosen to signify the common people." This contrast is economic as well as intellectual. " By

[1] *Works*, ed. 1851, vi, 8 seq.   [2] 9.   [3] 209.   [4] 211.

the common people we mean labourers, husbandmen, mechanics, and merchants in general, who pursue their occupations and industry without any knowledge in liberal arts or sciences, or in anything but their own trades and pursuits. . . . The gentlemen will ordinarily . . . be the richer" and " generally those who are rich and descended from families in public life will have the best education in arts and sciences." [1] But where class differences obtain, a class war must necessarily ensue : " In every society where property exists, there will ever be a struggle between rich and poor." [2] And this class war is of necessity a lasting state, because no party can succeed in gaining the upper hand : the forces are too equally divided. " The gentlemen in every country are, and ever must be, few in number, in comparison of the simplemen. . . . But the gentlemen are more intelligent and skilful, as well as generally richer and better connected, and therefore have more influence and power than an equal number of the common people." [3]

This equilibrium of class forces Adams wished to make the starting-point of practical politics. In its preservation he saw the best safeguard of social peace. This is why he rejected the one-chamber system. For where rich and poor are " mixed in one assembly, equal laws can never be expected : they will either be made by numbers, to plunder the few who are rich, or by influence, to fleece the many who are poor. Both rich and poor, then, must be made independent, that equal justice may be done, and equal liberty enjoyed by all. To expect that in a single sovereign assembly no load shall be laid upon any but what is common to all, nor to gratify the passions of any, but only to supply the necessities of their country, is altogether chimerical." [4] To the social must correspond a political equilibrium of forces. It acts in favour of the well-to-do, but this is in Adams' eyes a recommendation rather than a fault. " To give the people, uncontrolled, all the prerogatives and rights of supremacy, meaning the whole executive and judicial power, or even the whole undivided legislative, is not the way to preserve liberty. . . . It must be remembered that the rich are people as well as the poor ; that they have rights as well as others ; that they have as clear and as sacred a right to their large property as others have to theirs which is smaller ; that oppression to them is as possible, and as wicked, as to others ; that stealing, robbing, cheating, are the same crimes and sins, whether committed

[1] 185.   [2] 68.   [3] 185.   [4] 168 seq.

against them or others. The rich, therefore, ought to have an effectual barrier in the constitution against being robbed, plundered, and murdered, as well as the poor; and this can never be without an independent senate. The poor should have a bulwark against the same dangers and oppressions; and this can never be without a house of representatives of the people. But neither the rich nor the poor can be defended by their respective guardians in the constitution without any executive power, vested with a negative, equal to either, to hold the balance even between them, and to decide when they cannot agree." [1] Thus Adams in the end advocates the English system of division of powers. He favoured it because he was convinced that it best corresponded to the fundamental facts of human psychology. " Though we allow benevolence and generous affections to exist in the human breast, yet every moral theorist will admit the selfish passions in the generality of men to be the strongest. . . . Self-interest, private avidity, ambition, and avarice, will exist in every state of society, and under every form of government. . . . The only remedy is to take away the power, by controlling the selfish avidity of the governor, by the senate and house; of the senate, by the governor and house; and of the house, by the governor and senate." [2] This political organization of the body social is best, because it invests the best—that is to say, in John Adams' way of thinking, the richest—with dominion : " Patricians, nobles, senators, the aristocratical part of the community, call it by what name you please, are noble patriots when they are kept under; they are really then the best men and the best citizens. But there is no possibility of keeping them under but by giving them . . . two masters in a free government. One of the masters I mean is the executive power in the first magistrate, and the other is the people in their house of representatives. Under these two masters they are, in general, the best men, citizens, magistrates, generals, or other officers; they are the guardians, ornaments, and glory of the community." [3]

Thus John Adams' social philosophy is a glorification of the class state and a rejection of the state of equality—that state of equality which the European bourgeoisie had so admired in America. " No love of equality, at least since Adam's fall, even existed in human nature," he says. Therefore " no [social] democracy ever did or can exist ".[4] " Love of equality and love of the democracy " are in Adams' view no more than

[1] 88 seq., 65.   [2] 57 seq.   [3] 73.   [4] 210.

"fantastical passions, feigned for the regulation and animation of a government that never had a more solid existence than the flying island of Lagado." [1]

In one point only is Adams' great antagonist, John Taylor of Caroline, author of the *Inquiry into the Principles and Policy of the Government of the United States* (1814), at one with him : in the recognition of private property as the basis of society. " Property is surely a right of mankind as really as liberty," said the philosopher of Massachusetts.[2] " The moment the idea is admitted into society, that property is not as sacred as the laws of God, and that there is not a force of law and public justice to protect it, anarchy and tyranny commence." The same idea was expressed by the philosopher of Virginia in an equally emphatic way : " A love of property is the chief basis of civil society."[3]

The consequences, however, which Taylor drew from this basic attitude, are different from those of Adams. Protection of the richer against the poorer, is Adams' only concern, protection of the poorer against the richer, is Taylor's principal idea : " There are two modes of invading private property ; the first, by which the poor plunder the rich, is sudden and violent ; the second, by which the rich plunder the poor, slow and legal. . . . Whether the law shall gradually transfer the property of the many to the few, or insurrection shall rapidly divide the property of the few among the many, it is equally an invasion of private property, and equally contrary to our constitutions. If equalizing and accumulating laws are the same in principle, it is inconceivable how the same mind should be able to detest the one, and approve the other. Integrity is compelled to reject both."[4] Now it is not, as Adams pretends, that the rich have to protect themselves against the greed of the poor. On the contrary, the poor are forced to defend themselves against the avidity of the rich : " Governments were instituted to enable men to keep their property, but in these evil days they use public powers to transfer property from the owners to factitious, legally created special interest."[5]

Two kinds of property, Taylor emphasizes, must be distinguished : property that rests on labour, which is sacred, however far it may extend, and property that arises from monopolies or other privileges. This is evil, however confined it may be. There is " a rational and practicable distinction

---

[1] *Ib.* [2] 8 seq. [3] *Construction Construed* (1820), 29.
[4] *Inquiry*, 280. [5] 561.

between that species of private property founded only in law, such as is gained by privilege, hierarchy, paper, charter, and sinecure; and that founded also in nature, arising from industry, arts, and sciences".[1] Only possessions coming from these sources are morally beyond reproach. Their prototype is landed property: "Land is not created by law.... It does not subsist upon other interests ... nor can it be corrupted except by laws which confine lands to a minority."[2] Wealth artificially created, however, is the mainspring of all evil: "From the legal frauds by which property is transferred and amassed, human nature has derived most of its envy, malice, and hatred."[3] Are the United States to be and to remain a democracy, not only in name, but also in fact? If so, natural property alone must be protected which never leads far from equality; artificial property, however, repressed, because it makes masters and slaves. "If wealth is accumulated into the hands of a few, either by a feudal or a stock monopoly, it carries the power also; and a government becomes as certainly aristocratical, by a monopoly of wealth, as by a monopoly of arms. A minority, obtaining a majority of wealth or arms in any mode, becomes the government."[4] The practical implication is clear: "A division of wealth is a necessary auxiliary to a division of power; and an accumulation of the former a stride towards rendering the latter useless."[5] "Wealth, like suffrage, must be considerably distributed, to sustain a democratick republick."[6]

In this opinion centres the essential difference between Taylor and Adams. Adams regarded the class division of society as a necessity of nature, and suggested rendering it harmless by establishing an equilibrium of class forces in the sense of Shaftesbury and Mably. Taylor denied the natural necessity of a class division of society and upheld as specifically American the egalitarian principle—the principle of the equilibrium of individual forces " by balancing man with man ". The crux of the whole discussion is obviously the decision of the question: is the class division of society a necessity of nature?

Adams, when he answered this question in the affirmative, referred to the age-long experience of mankind which is laid down in universal history. For where do we find a nation that has not been split into classes? Taylor does not deny what to deny is impossible. But he draws the opposite conclusions from the facts of the past: an unprejudiced analysis of universal

[1] 564. [2] 260. [3] 563. [4] 275. [5] 325. [6] 274.

history, he asserts, establishes beyond doubt that the origin of class differences was always due to artificial interference and never, as John Adams believed, to natural tendencies.

In the oldest times the clergy occupied the position of the dominant class. What was the basis of their power? Men's childish fear of the wrath of God, continually kept alive in them. The priests possessed an artificial " monopoly of souls ". They were an " Aristocracy of superstition ". In the Middle Ages the feudal lords became the leading social stratum. Their claim to the usurpation of dominion was the pretended necessity of protecting nation and state. The knights had an artificial " monopoly of land ". They were an " aristocracy of conquest ". After the defeat of the second and first estate by the bourgeoisie it would well have been possible to leave things to their natural development, and, had this been done, an ideal order of liberty and equality would have arisen. But mankind was again fooled by a small group of privileged egoists. After the sanction of God and the sanction of war it is the sanction of statute books, i.e., the sanction of legal privileges, which serves to divide society into hostile camps. The dominant class of the " third age " rests on a " monopoly of money ". It is an " aristocracy of paper and patronage ". Against it Taylor takes the field with the moral conviction and political postulate that labour and property must not be separated. " Our policy is founded upon the idea, that it is both wise and just, to leave the distribution of property to industry and talents ; that what they acquire is all their own, except what they owe to society ; that they owe nothing to society except a contribution equivalent to the necessities of government ; that they owe nothing to monopoly or exclusive privilege in any form ; and that whether they are despoiled by the rage of a mob, or the laws of a separate interest, the genuine sanction of private property is equally violated." [1]

To this programme the programme of the " money-ocracy " is diametrically opposed : " Our purpose ", so Taylor expresses it, " is to settle wealth and power upon a minority. It will be accomplished by national debt, paper corporations, and offices, civil and military. These will condense king, lords, and commons, a monied faction and an armed faction, in one interest. This interest must subsist upon another, or perish. The other interest is national, to govern and pilfer which is our object, and

[1] 282.

its accomplishment consists in getting the utmost a nation can pay." [1]

These shameless intentions can only be realized if legislation becomes subservient to them. Taylor is firmly convinced that, where *laissez-faire* exists, no upper class can arise. For where *laissez-faire* obtains, tendencies are at work continually to re-establish the continually disturbed equilibrium of individual forces. In economic life free competition prevents the accumulation of excessive wealth ; in intellectual life a wide popular education breaks any temporary monopoly of knowledge.

But alas ! in the United States there is no *laissez-faire*. In the United States all the endeavours of the federal power are directed towards forming, and making all-powerful, a small group of masters. All Taylor's writing—and he was a profuse writer—served the one great aim, irrefutably to establish this thesis.

As early as 1794, in his pamphlet *Definition of Parties*, Taylor had put forward the assertion that the legislation of Congress had singled out five thousand individuals of the five millions of inhabitants of the United States in order to constitute and privilege them as the " paper interest ". " The general government has been an exclamation for money, more money. Obliterate from the statute book all laws in favour of paper, and the code would be almost a blank. It exhibits a succession of new burdens upon the five millions which are a succession of delicious repast to the five thousand." [2] Especially Hamilton's " laws divided the nation into a minority enriched, and a majority furnishing the riches ; and two parties, seekers and defenders of wealth, are an unavoidable consequence." [3]

What means were employed by the governing clique to reach their base end ? " The original funding system, subsequent loans, a flood of bank currency, the bankruptcy of some banks, and the refusal or inability of all to pay their debts, the extravagance of our governments, loans, pensions, and the great increase of protecting duties, in many cases amounting to a prohibition, are so many instruments for cutting off species of property from industry, to enrich capitalists, as the Abyssinian fattens himself with steaks cut from living cows." [4] The new time is worse than the old. " We got rid of tythes, and now we clasp banks, patronage, and protecting duties to our bosoms. Ten per centum upon labour was paid to a priesthood, forming a body of men which extended knowledge, and cultivated good

[1] 40. [2] *Ib*. [3] *Inquiry*, 569. [4] *Tyranny Unmasked* (1822), 92.

morals, as some compensation for forming also a legal faction, guided by the spirit of encroachment upon the rights and property of the majority. Forty per centum is now paid on our labour, to a legal faction guided by the same spirit, and pretending to no religion, to no morality, to no patriotism, except to the religion, morality, and patriotism of making itself daily richer." [1]

The American republics have removed the great dangers of feudal oppression, but only to give free course to the greater dangers of capitalist class dictatorship. " The Americans devoted their effectual precautions to the obsolete modes of title and hierarchy, erected several barriers against the army mode, and utterly disregarded the mode of paper and patronage. The army mode was thought so formidable that military men are excluded from legislatures and limited to charters and commissions at will; and the paper mode so harmless, that it is allowed to break the principle of keeping legislative, executive, and judicative powers separate and distinct, to infuse itself into all these departments, to unite them in one conspiracy, and to obtain charters or commissions for unrestricted terms, entrenched behind publick faith, and out of the reach, it is said, of national will; which it may assail, wound, and destroy with impunity. This jealousy of armies and confidence in paper system can only be justified, if the following argument of defence is correct : . . . Soldiers, admitted to the legislature, would legislate in favour of soldiers; but stock jobbers will not legislate in favour of stock jobbers." [2]

Thus the door is open to great evil; and greater evil will arise therefrom. " As paper property is accumulated, the leisure and income of the holders will be increased. The weight of talent will follow leisure and wealth. . . . This superiority of talents and wealth will invest individuals . . . with an influence well calculated to acquire an ascendancy over the landed interest." [3] It will not be long before the war of the cunning plutocrats against the simple peasantry will resemble the war of a " veteran army " against an " undisciplined militia ". [4] And what will be the consequence? " A legislature, in a nation where the system of paper and patronage prevails, will be governed by that interest, and legislate in its favour. It is impossible to do this without legislating to the injury of the other

---

[1] *Arator*, 35 seq., cit. Mudge, *The Social Philosophy of John Taylor of Caroline* (1939), 161.
[2] *Inquiry*, 42.   [3] 262.   [4] 388.

interest, that is, the great mass of the nation. Such a legislature will create unnecessary offices, that themselves or their relations may be endowed with them. They will lavish the revenue to enrich themselves. They will borrow for the nation that they may lend. They will offer lenders great profits that they may share in them." [1] The evils of artificial inequality will oust the benefits of natural equality. No longer will Europe's philosophers admire and envy America's happiness.

Against the dangers of capitalism, the dangers of paper and patronage, John Taylor fought valiantly. He did not doubt the justice of his enterprise and its possibility. " All societies have exercised the right of abolishing privileged, stipendary or factitious property, whenever they became detrimental to them." [2] He could not and would not believe that the old dream of a community of equals was gone for ever. But it was too late. The class contrast was already too deep. " I fear", Thomas Jefferson wrote in 1824 to Robert J. Garnett,[3] " it is the voice of one crying in the wilderness." The United States went the way which John Adams, the great realist, had predicted and foreseen. The forebodings of Raynal and Mably, Chastellux and Brissot, came true.

Thus even in the New World the ideal of equality found no home. Thus even America became a country of social conflicts. And how could it have been otherwise ? Nothing human is perfect. The ideal is like the polar star : it leads man through the night, but is as far now from this earth as on the seventh day.

[1] 39.   [2] 562.
[3] *The Writings of Thomas Jefferson*, ed. Washington, 1854, VII, 336.

INDEX

Abolition, see Slavery, Abolition of
Adams, John, 49, 101-7, 110
Adams, Samuel, 73 sq.
Agriculture, 21, 25-7, 30, 32, 51 sq., 54, 65, 69, 73, 90-2, 96 sq., 99
—, see also Soil, Thuenen's scheme
America and Americans, see United States
Anarchy, 46, 105
Aristocracy, 46 sq., 49-52, 54, 57, 69, 72-4, 91, 98, 104, 106 sq.
—, see also Bourgeoisie ; Democracy ; Feudalism ; Landlords
Artizans, see Bourgeoisie
Arts, 21, 27, 34, 76, 78 sq., 92 sq., 103, 106
—, see also Culture ; Music ; Science
Ascent, Social and economic, Possibility of, 24, 27, 34, 41, 48, 50, 52, 67, 70-2, 89
—, see also Equality

Baltimore, 79
Bastiat, Frédéric, 6
Bentham, Jeremy, 14, 73
Blacks, see Negroes
Bohemia, 30
Bolingbroke, Henry Saint-John, 2
Boston, 30, 52, 79, 92, 94, 96
Bourgeoisie, 2, 8-12, 14, 22, 52, 66 sq., 75, 80, 92, 96 sq., 99, 104, 107
—, see also Aristocracy ; Capitalism ; Cities ; Commerce ; Democracy
Brissot de Warville, Jean Pierre, 15, 80, 81-100, 101, 110

Calvin, Jean, 40
Capitalism, 10-12, 14, 38, 43, 53, 70, 101, 108-10
—, see also Bourgeoisie ; Communism ; Socialism
Carey, Henry Charles, 6
Carolina, 29 sq., 69
—, South, 28
Charlestown, 79

Chastellux, François-Jean de, 15, 58-79, 80-2, 92, 94, 96, 101, 110
China, 25
Cities, 9, 18, 28, 54, 65, 78 sq., 90, 93, 96-8, 100
—, see also Baltimore ; Boston ; Charlestown ; Geneva ; Jamestown ; Lisbon ; London ; New York ; Philadelphia ; Turnbull City in Florida ; Williamsburgh
Civil war, 1861-5, 30
Class contrast, 31, 34, 41, 44, 46 sq., 50 sq., 54 sq., 67-9, 72-6, 87, 91 sq., 97, 101 sq., 106-10
— —, see also Ascent, Possibility of ; Bourgeoisie ; Capitalism ; Proletariat
— state, 52, 57, 72, 101 sq., 104
— struggle, 24, 54, 101, 103
Classical economics, 6
Commerce, 21, 23, 26 sq., 32, 51-4, 56 sq., 63, 65, 73, 79, 96-8
—, see also Cities
Communism, 12, 37 sq., 42 sq., 88
—, see also Bourgeoisie ; Capitalism ; Proletariat
Congress, 56, 93, 101, 108
—, see also Constitutions, American ; Representatives, American ; Senate
Connecticut, 29, 70 sq., 91 sq.
Constitution, British, see Political power, Division of
Constitutions, American, 49, 54, 56, 73 sq., 104 sq.
—, see also Congress ; Federal power ; Senate
Creation, 82 sq.
—, Plan of, 4
Culture, 18, 76-9, 92 sq., 96 sq., 99
—, see also Art ; Music ; Science
Custom, 18, 57, 64 sq., 91
—, see also Manners, Simplicity of

Deism, 2
Delaware, 92

111

INDEX

Democracy, 19, 27, 46 sq., 49, 51 sq., 54, 68 sq., 71, 73–5, 98, 104, 106
—, see also Aristocracy ; Bourgeoisie ; Constitutions, American ; Political power, Distribution of
Descartes, René, 37, 68
Development, see Progress
Diderot, Denis, 16
Distribution, see Wealth
Dryden, John, 2

Earthquake, see Lisbon
Economics, Classical, see Classical economics
Education, 37, 108
Egalitarianism, 10 sq., 96, 99, 101, 106
—, see also Equality
Egoism, see Selfishness
Emigration, 90, 92
—, see also West, American, Trek to
Employment, see Labour
England, 14 sq., 50, 52, 67 sq., 74 sq.
Enlightenment, see Reason
Entelechy, 3
Equality, 10, 14, 21–6, 28, 32–4, 36–46, 48–52, 54, 61, 65, 69, 72 sq., 75, 87–9, 92, 101 sq., 104, 106 sq., 110
—, see also Ascent, Possibility of ; Equilibrium ; Harmony ; Inequality ; Liberty ; Manners, Simplicity of
Equilibrium, 11, 40, 46 sq., 49, 52, 56, 68 sq., 87, 103, 106, 108
—, see also Class contrast ; Political power, Division of
Europe, 14 sq., 25, 27 sq., 31, 33, 44, 48 sq., 53, 55, 70, 72, 76, 78, 80, 86, 89 sq., 92–4, 98 sq., 104, 110
—, see also England ; France ; Germany ; Sweden ; Switzerland
Evil, 2–6, 8, 12, 18 sq., 23, 37–9, 41–4, 62, 64–6, 106, 109
—, see also Morals ; Selfishness ; Virtue

Fatalism, see Raynal
Federal power, 108
Federalists, 101

Feudalism, 14 sq., 97, 109
—, see also Landlords ; Soil
Feugère, Anatole, 16
Fine arts, see Arts
France, 14 sq., 75–80, 88, 90
Fraternity, see Harmony
Free will, 3 sq.
Frugality, see Manners, Simplicity of
Funerals, 28
—, see also Luxury

Garnett, Robert J., 110
Geneva, 40
George III, King, 15
Georgia, 53
Germany, 14 sq.
God, 2–7, 9, 11, 14
Good, see Evil
Government, 18, 20 sq., 27, 45–7, 49–52, 56, 58, 62–4, 68 sq., 71–3, 90, 100, 104–8
—, see also Aristocracy ; Constitutions, American ; Democracy ; Political power, Division of
Governor, 74
Griffin, Cyrus, *President of Congress*, 93

Hamilton, Alexander, 101, 108
Happiness, 4 sq., 10 sq., 14, 17–22, 24, 26 sq., 33, 36, 38, 41–4, 53, 59–61, 63–5, 67, 69, 75, 78 sq., 91, 93, 96, 98, 100, 110
—, see also Equality ; Harmony ; Liberty
Happiness, Greatest, of greatest number, 58
Harmony, 6 sq., 10, 12, 22, 26, 28, 34, 38 sq., 41 sq., 46, 49, 53 sq., 61 sq., 67 sq., 71, 73–5, 100, 103
—, see also Harmony, Pre-established
—, Pre-established, 6, 10
Holbach, Paul Heinrich Dietrich, Baron D', 16
Hutcheson, Francis, 6

Independence, 53, 93
—, War of, 69
Individualism, 85, 96
—, see also Liberty

INDEX

Industrial revolution, 10
Industry, 26 sq., 30, 52, 54, 63 sq., 66, 71, 90 sq., 98–100, 106, 108
—, see also Commerce
Inequality, 10 sq., 14, 17, 23 sq., 27–9, 32, 34, 36 sq., 40, 42, 44 sq., 48 sq., 53, 62 sq., 65, 68, 72 sq., 75, 88 sq., 92, 98 sq., 110
—, see also Ascent, Possibility of ; Class contrast ; Equality ; Harmony ; Liberty ; Political power, Distribution of ; Wealth
Inheritance, Law of, 45
—, Right of, 25
Injustice, 21, 45, 50
—, see also Justice
Innate ideas, 37
Inquisition, 64
Interests, Artificial identification of, 73

James-town, 29
Jefferson, Thomas, *President*, 101, 110
Justice, 38 sq., 103, 105
—, see also Injustice ; Legislation

Kant, Immanuel, 14

Labour, 22, 24, 30, 33, 44, 48, 52 sq., 66, 70, 80, 87, 89 sq., 92 sq., 97, 99, 105, 107
—, see also Capitalism ; Industry ; Proletariat ; Wage-earners
Lacedæmon, see Sparta
Lagrange, Joseph Louis, 16
Land, see Soil
Landlords, 14 sq., 25, 47, 50, 52, 71, 73, 75 sq., 79 sq., 92, 104, 107
—, see also Feudalism
Language, 77
Laski, Harold J., 36
Latifundium, 45
Law, see Legislation
Laws, Sumptuary, see Sumptuary laws
Laziness, see Evil
Legislation, 23 sq., 33, 39, 42, 45 sq., 48, 54–6, 62, 64 sq., 71, 89, 100, 105 sq., 108, 110
—, see also Government
—, English, 67

Leibniz, Gottfried Wilhelm, 2–10, 12
Liberalism, 22, 97
—, see also Liberty
Liberty, 3, 14, 18, 21 sq., 24 sq., 27 sq., 32 sq., 35–8, 40 sq., 47 sq., 50 sq., 56, 68 sq., 79, 100 sq., 103, 105, 107
—, see also Equality ; Free will ; Individualism
Lincoln, Abraham, 29
Lisbon, Earthquake of, 1, 7–9
Locke, John, 47, 69
London, 30, 58, 100
Luxury, 17, 26, 28 sq., 33–5, 40, 55 sq., 63, 80, 91 sq., 95–7, 99
—, see also Cities ; Manners, Simplicity of ; Sumptuary laws ; Women
Lycurgus, see Sparta

Mably, Gabriel Bonnot de, 15, 36–57, 58 sq., 63, 69, 82, 101, 106, 110
Maddison, James, *Professor, of Williamsburgh*, 72 sq., 79
Malebranche, Nicole, 37
Manners, 78
—, Simplicity of, 27 sq., 32, 34, 38–40, 51, 53, 55, 69, 91 sq., 95, 97
—, —, see also Custom
Manufacture, see Industry
Maryland, 92
Massachusetts, 29, 51 sq., 73
Mazzei, Filippo, 48
Mediocrity, see Bourgeoisie ; Manners, Simplicity of
Middle Ages, 2, 11, 107
—, see also Feudalism
Mill, James, 10 sq.
Monarchy, 46 sq., 68
Monopoly, 105–8
Montesquieu, Charles de, 30
Morals, 81, 91, 94, 98, 100
—, see also Manners ; Manners, Simplicity of
Motion, 82 sq., 85
Music, 78, 94 sq.

Nature, 9, 23, 25, 37 sq., 44, 60 sq., 78, 84–8, 106

114   INDEX

Nature, see also Order
—, Law of, 4, 11, 20, 24, 36, 48, 60, 88
—, State of, 17-19, 28, 59-61, 86 sq.
—, Human, 40, 43 sq., 61, 91, 102, 104
—, —, see also Free will
Needs, 33, 39-41, 84-9, 91, 96
—, Artificial, 53, 55, 87
—, —, see also Manners, Simplicity of
Negroes, 48, 72, 76, 92
—, see also Slavery
New England, 29 sq., 72, 77, 91
New Jersey, 70, 78
New York, 97
Nobility, see Landlords
Nobles, see Landlords

Optimism, Philosophical, see Leibniz
Order, 3 sq., 6, 8, 84, 95
—, see also Harmony, Nature
—, Natural, 36, 86 sq.
—, Social, 86

Pain, 4, 18, 26, 60, 67
—, see also Suffering
Paraguay, Jesuit state of, 21 sq.
Pauw, Cornelius de, 15
Peace, Social, see Harmony
Peasants, see Bourgeoisie
Penn, William, 33, 69, 96
Pennsylvania, 33, 51 sq., 69, 93, 100
People, 50, 76, 103 sq.
—, see also Population
—, Supremacy of, 54 sq.
—, —, see also Democracy
Pessimism, Philosophical, see Mably, Schopenhauer
Philadelphia, 52, 76, 78 sq., 96
Philosophers, Scottish, 6
Physiocrats, 6, 25
Plato, 46 sq., 88
Pleasure, see Pain
Political power, Division of, 46 sq., 68, 103 sq., 106 sq., 109
—, see also Congress ; Constitutions, American ; Government ; Representatives, American ; Senate
Poor, The, see Rich, The
Pope, Alexander, 2, 7

Population, 24, 26, 28 sq., 31, 54, 75, 89 sq., 96, 99 sq.
Price, Richard, 15
Primitive man, see Savage
Progress, 2, 12, 18, 58, 61, 63-7
Proletariat, 48, 52 sq., 89, 101
—, see also Labour, Wage-earners
Property, 21-4, 26-8, 32-4, 37, 41-3, 51-3, 55, 66, 69, 73-5, 83-90, 93, 97 sq., 100, 102 sq., 105-10
—, see also Wealth
—, Landed, 45, 75, 89, 106
—, Right of, 84, 87, 109
Prosperity, see Wealth
Public debt, 101
— welfare, 40

Quakers, 51, 76 sq., 94-6
Quesnay, François, 6, 25

Rationalism, see Reason
Raynal, Guillaume-Thomas, 15, 16-35, 36, 40, 45 sq., 59, 82, 101, 110
—, His collaborators, 16
Reason, 2, 59, 65, 69
Religion, 25, 91
Representatives, American, 51 sq., 73, 104
—, see also Congress ; Democracy ; Government ; Senate
— of the people, 74
Republicanism, 92
Republicans, 101
Revolution, French, 16
Rich, The, 23 sq., 33, 36, 42, 44, 50, 52, 54-7, 69, 72, 75, 87-9, 96, 101, 103-5
—, see also Property ; Wealth
Riches, see Wealth
Rousseau, Jean Jacques, 8-11, 16-18, 37, 75

Saint-Lambert, Jean François, Marquis de, 16
Savage, 17-19, 23, 32, 60 sq., 63, 65, 71, 85 sq.
Schérer, Edmond, 16
Schopenhauer, Arthur, 12
Science, 21, 64, 92, 96, 103, 106

INDEX

Scottish philosophers, *see* Philosophers, Scottish
Selfishness, 6, 11 sq., 104
—, *see also* Evil ; Virtue
Senate, 49, 52, 74, 104
—, *see also* Congress ; Representatives, American
Settlers, *see* Population
Shaftesbury, Anthony, Earl of, 2, 106
Simplicity, *see* Manners, Simplicity of
Sin, 4
—, *see also* Evil ; Selfishness ; Virtue
Slavery, 29-32, 48, 72, 76, 91 sq., 94, 99 sq.
—, *see also* Negroes
—, Abolition of, 29, 32
Smith, Adam, 6 sq., 10
Socialism, 12, 22, 38
—, *see also* Communism ; Proletariat
Soil, 54, 72, 97, 99
—, *see also* Agriculture ; Property ; Wealth
—, Equal division of, 42
—, Monopoly of, 15, 72
—, Price of, 90, 93, 99
—, Private property of, 37, 70
—, Social distinction in property of, 47
Soul-unit, *see* Entelechy
Sparta, 34, 39 sq., 44, 47, 49, 63, 69, 88
Suffering, 3 sq., 64, 95
—, *see also* Pain
Sumptuary laws, 40, 45, 55
—, *see also* Luxury
Sweden, 47
Switzerland, 27 sq.

Taxation, 101
Taylor, John, of Caroline, 101, 105-10
Temperance, *see* Manners, Simplicity of
Théodicée, 3
Third estate, *see* Bourgeoisie
Thuenen's scheme, 30
Toleration, 2, 100
Towns, *see* Cities
Trade, *see* Commerce
Turgot, Anne Robert Jacques, Baron de Laune, 6

Turnbull City in Florida, 34
Tyranny, 18, 20, 23, 27, 31 sq., 45 sq., 51, 88, 105
—, *see also* Government

United States, 14 sq., 21, 24, 28-34, 47-57, 69-81, 86, 89-93, 97-110
— —, Contrast between North and South, 30 sq., 72, 91 sq.
— —, Northern, 71 sq., 76, 94, 96 sq.
— —, Southern, 72, 76, 92-4
— —, *see also* Carolina ; Connecticut ; Delaware ; Georgia ; Maryland ; Massachusetts ; New England ; New Jersey ; Pennsylvania ; Virginia ; West, Trek to
Universe, 3 sq., 6, 83 sq., 86
—, *see also* Creation
Utility, 2, 97

Vice, *see* Virtue
Virginia, 29 sq., 71 sq., 76, 91-4, 99 sq.
Virtue, 19, 21, 25 sq., 33, 38 sq., 53-5, 57, 78, 92, 94 sq., 97-9
—, *see also* Evil ; Happiness
Voltaire, François Marie Arouet de, 7-9, 16

Wage-earners, 48, 66, 70
—, *see also* Bourgeoisie ; Capitalism ; Industry ; Labour ; Proletariat
Wants, *see* Needs
War of all against all, 62, 84
Washington, George, *President*, 29, 101
Wealth, 11, 26-8, 33, 35, 37 sq., 40-2, 45, 47, 50-6, 65, 67, 73, 76, 86, 89, 93, 96-8, 106-9
—, *see also* Aristocracy ; Industry ; Inequality ; Luxury ; Property
—, Distribution of, 89, 92, 101, 106
West, American, Trek to, 28
—, *see also* Emigration ; Population
Whitfield, E. A., 43
Williamsburgh, 29, 72
—, *see also* Maddison, Professor
Women, 34, 56, 80, 93-5, 97
—, *see also* Arts ; Luxury ; Music